CULTURAL DIFFERENCES OR DISCRIMINATION?

J I Suleri

iUniverse, Inc.
New York Bloomington

Cultural Differences or Discrimination?

iUniverse books may be ordered through booksellers or by contacting:

iUniverse
1663 Liberty Drive
Bloomington, IN 47403
www.iuniverse.com
1-800-Authors (1-800-288-4677)

ISBN: 978-0-595-52250-7 (pbk)
ISBN: 978-0-595-62305-1 (ebk)

Printed in the United States of America

Contents

1. Overview   1

2. Human Psychology   23

3. Role of Elders   28

4. Human Wishes   31

5. Within Culture Inequity   35

6. Behavioral Approach   39

7. Pretending Unselfishness   43

8. Another Angle of Prejudice   46

9. Other Ways of Classification   49

10. Role of Bureaucracy   54

11. Concept of Freedom   59

12. How Young Blacks Feel   64

13. Trust in Relationships   69

14. Long Hair Small Brains   73

15. Fighting For Satisfaction   76

16. Human Intelligence   80

17. What A Difference   84

18. Rapid Changes   88

19. What A Contrast   92

20. Sense of Responsibility   96

21. Miserable Liberty   100

22. Another Phase of Liberty   105

23. Life Sacrifice   111

24. Union is Strength   115

25. What Are Rights   119

26. Revenge or Intolerance   123

27. What Is Truth   130

28. No Blame Game   133

29. Power of Love and Concord   136

30. Respect for All   139

31. United We Stand   143

CULTURAL DIFFERENCES OR DISCRIMINATION?
AN OVERVIEW

I T HAS OFTEN BEEN SAID that the Westerners do not like the people from the Second or Third world, and most of the time the rest of the world has given them different titles such as discriminators, racists, fascists etc. And all the time they have to clarify their position, but has anybody ever thought that people from those parts have their valid arguments or are they just using human values? Since it is evident that they thought they have been used by the Westerners in the former times and now it is their right to use their facilities. Now who's right is what, and how can we determine this seems very confusing to me. But it looks like a 'tit for tat' competition in the World. It was hard for me to understand the difference or whatever in the beginning. Since I was brought up in the Eastern culture and lived in the Western culture I have noticed life in a very unique way. I have seen different colors and different cultures but at the same time I have noticed that people from every where are the same and there is only one race in this world - the human race. I am getting the privilege to write some of my observations and amazing contrasts between human beings.

While I was in Sydney I spent all my days calculating and making plans that after completing my studies I would go back home and live the rest of my life with my people. I continuously wrote letters and always anxiously waited for replies. My family always replied, but from others, letters were scarce. I realized that I was expecting too much from them and certainly was as important to them as before. Well I had to be more realistic and realize; 'Out of sight, out of mind'. On the first stage of my itinerary: from Karachi to Bangkok on Thai Airways I observed a very interesting incident which I would put down to inherent human behavior. Now I do not want to go into nationalities. Sitting next to me was an Asian, probably from the South Eastern part who apparently had not understood the announcement to fasten the seatbelts. This gentleman had put his seat cushion on his knee and the air hostess checked everyone's belt with a quick glance but missed the gentleman next to me. I cannot say I was the only one aware of his position but at least I knew he had not fastened his belt, it could be the fact he had completely forgotten but with his body language I figured out that he did not know how to clip the belt. I could feel his embarrassment and could easily empathize with his feelings as well. Opting not to add to his embarrassment, what I did was to open my own seat belt and start playing with it. I was watching him the whole time, and finally he successfully fastened his own seat belt.

In some Asian countries, use of the traditional knife and fork is not in custom. Now at the time when the Air line staff finally decided to bless the people with the prescribed food and with their sophisticated utensils (though mostly they are made of very thin quality plastic rather fine quality) a few people were uncomfortable with the fork, knife combination. As the saying goes,' practice makes a man perfect' these people having had no practice whatsoever of using the knife fork combination, were thus eating with obvious discomfort and what really astonished me was that none of them had asked or even enquired about the spoons which I believe was definitely their right. I curiously watched them and I heard someone whisper in their local language which coincidently was familiar to me, and hence I am getting the privilege to translate, "It is YUK to eat with a knife and fork".

Here what really disturbed me, why did these people force themselves to eat their meal in a fashion they were not used to, when they could have eaten comfortably simply by asking for spoons. They had to pretend to be able to eat with the combination comfortably and to me the question here is WHY? Why do they have to behave like this? The answer comes to my mind, yes it is quite human to pretend to be what we are not supposed to be; but it was not only their behavior which compels me to think about that particular human attitude. It is happening all the day every day around us, but since we are not directly suffering we are not taking that factor so seriously, whereas sometimes by talking with each other people can solve a lot of matters rather then to keep pretending that they are perfect, but the true reality is "nobody is perfect". One can always try to work hard to be a perfect according to one's own standards but that does not say that one's perfectionism is suitable for others as well. Can we think about that sometimes?

Soon we landed at the Hong Kong Airport. I had no idea about the people of H.K. Whenever I used to see anyone from the Far East, I would presume him to be Chinese. For me to distinguish among the people of the Far East countries is difficult as it would be for any European to distinguish among the sub-continental people, he would always think them to be Indian. I had to stay at Hong Kong for ten hours, in such a situation I was very confident but nervous as well and tried to calm myself in advance. Where there is a language barrier there is always a communication problem. It is not a problem at the Airport itself, but outside I would say God's special blessings be on the tourists. What I found most interesting was that while speaking with other people, even if you abuse them, they would go on smiling. I thought may be they are stupid or they are making fools of the other people. After a detailed observation, I came to the conclusion that they are very good-natured and clever human beings, and by giving meaningless smiles, actually they were hiding their language barrier. This they might have learned from the English, since I have noticed that at embarrassing moments an Englishman will behave quite nicely which I believe might lessen the intensity of the embarrassment. And of course in 150 years there should be some English influence on them.

My next stop was at Bangkok, about which I had heard a lot and I decided to stay there for a while. I had been told Bangkok is a paradise, but believe me it is a paradise only for the certain class with a rather unique frame of mind. If the definition of paradise is a place where there are no restrictions at all - then Bangkok with no "SEX" restrictions is certainly a paradise. There I found most tourists wanting to know where the paradise was. I would say, it is a nice country to tour and watch the frustrated people of the world. Amazing isn't it? I would say it is good to go there for a change and acquire new experiences. I certainly had my experience while touring there - not to believe in rumors.

The next day I flew to Sydney, my final destination of the tour, where I planned to stay quite a while. At the Airport the customs' officer, a lady, while examining my luggage asked me questions, which I believe is a part of their duty as well as public relations. She asked me the purpose of my stay in Australia, I replied that I was planning to study further and I had been admitted in one of the recognized universities in Sydney. She guided me to finding the way to the youth hostel and she behaved very nicely in all ways. After the clearance she gave me a reason to revise my opinion about the customs people around the world. Having heard of their notoriety, I was pleasantly surprised with this officer's behavior. And I feel no hesitation to say that she was the first Aussie, who had given me a very good impression of the country. I do not know whether I can recognize her now or whether she remembered me particularly, but my intentions are to write about her positive behavior and to communicate to others that sometimes only one good experience can have a good impact on a human being's life.

From the Immigration cell I went to the Tourism department office for more information about the Sydney city, where I obtained some very practical advices and a city map. Thus fully armed I entered the city, and I took a cab to the Youth Hostel which was in the Glebe. I had always thought myself to be very adjustable person, but after staying one night at the hostel, I felt totally left out. Being summer time, there were many tourists from different parts of the world who were staying and since they were new there as well, I could see them hesitating to invite a communication. I was also quite reserved in what was to me a strange environment. Also I had to be very careful about my meals, since my up bringing was in the part of the world where pork meat was rarely available and I had certain other obligations about the food. It was very awkward for me to keep enquiring about the ingredients of the food whereas it seemed to me other people were not really bothered. I managed three days at the hostel, and finally got my own apartment on rent. I am very thankful to the hostel staff for keeping an activity book, since I got the address and the telephone of my apartment from that book.

The night I had rented the apartment, I could not sleep and kept thinking about my decision to live apart and the time to come. It was the usual practice for the landlord to clean and furnish the apartment on renting it, and my landlord told me that all the work would take a week. I wanted to move as soon as possible and to him it was obviously a good surprise. I told him that I would do all the work since I had the time. I moved on that very day to my new home with fully satisfied with my first negotiation.

I next focused on another problem; I was living alone and had to do all the household chores, something I had never done before. In Pakistan, it is not the usual practice of a man to cook, clean and do the washing, and I never ventured to cook and wash in my life. Also, I was the youngest one in the family and that doubled with the fact of being a "MAN", had totally exempted me from such activities. Now, at this time, I had to study and perform all the necessary cooking and cleaning. I started thinking about my life back home; I had been employed in a multinational firm in the administration division and was thus in the habit of giving orders. And here, there was no one to even listen to me! I reconsider my decision of coming here and wondered whether it would be better to go back home. Finally, I pulled myself together and fought with myself. I concentrated on adjusting myself in that new society. Since my apartment was directly opposite the Youth Hostel, I started using the hostel facilities. My life revolved around studying, cooking and washing. Gradually I realized that this work was certainly good. I also noticed that with the change in my approach and thinking, I started making friends. One such friendship started in the laundry room which later turned out to be my best friendship in Australia. I now understand more and more the language, culture and the approach of those people towards practical life. Furthermore I would say what I have learned within a year by living with the locals, I have my great doubts that I would have only been able to learn in five years or more if I would have stuck to my own community or cult.

I had always thought myself to be a very independent person in Pakistan, but now I realized how dependent I used to be. I also do realize that the word independent itself is quite difficult to explain and I believe that no one is really independent in this world, everyone is dependent to each other in one way or another. This is an important factor in any religion as well for it is the basic factor of humanity to help each other and especially to be there for your friends and loved ones. My question here is whether we are practicing our beliefs what we really believe or it is just a show. I had found my answer by associating with the people of different countries, certainly with my other countries' friends. And I believe everyone can find the remedy by just being honest and sincere to one's own belief, and I am sure the beliefs on this earth teach us not to be quarrelsome and inhuman. Therefore if our teachings are positive, which everyone of us claims to believe, then why can we not live positively with each other.

Living in Sydney was to me a new cultural experience too, and I found it difficult. If you put anything new in front of a child, he will go for it irrespective of whether it is good or bad. Before analyzing it, he can not decide anything. My position was the same and I wanted to see and feel the culture before evaluating it. Just like when Moses touched the fire without thinking about the consequences and had to pay a huge price, since he had hurt his tongue and stuttered his whole life. So if the born leader (without doubts) can make mistakes just to learn more, then I believe I have every reason to follow them. To understand culture naturally is a matter of living in the heart of the society and associating with the people. In the culture which I have inherited, there are restrictions in the free mixing of both genders. It is a man-bashing culture, like most of the rest of the world but it has quite a bad reputation in the Western world. Male and female both have different rights and naturally they have different life privileges. I feel no hesitation in writing that people are not happy with the system, though the system itself has not as many flaws as it looks but the imposers have unnecessary powers and there is no independent solid check on them, since they themselves are the checkers as well. They have made it very hard for the people to even depart from the structure. In some cases they make power groups themselves and amend the law rather constitution to the way they want them and in the eyes of the public they are taking care of them. In other words there is a limitation of thought over there, and life is full of restrictions. The Western world is not really familiar with the 'word' restriction, apart from their traffic laws and on the entry of the other countries' people. Whereas these restrictions are rarely to be found in my homeland or even in the neighboring countries.

To the people of both cultures one factor is certainly common, that there are always the explorers and the frustrated people. To me it is the people who explore and acquire knowledge, who have a very positive approach irrespective of the culture they belong to. It is such people who are always open-minded and always have the chance to prosper in any society. But why and where does frustration enter? I would venture to explain why. In the Eastern culture and in Pakistan as well, living with numerous rules and regulations does make the people fed up and intolerant. They feel it is unfair to live in a stifled environment and would definitely like to exceed the limits set on them by society itself. They feel that they can not have freedom of speech, of thought or even of religion and that is why they are victims of frustration. Such people then turn to the other cultures and adopt them to some extent. Here comes the problem once again in their lives that they can not adjust and justify themselves thoroughly to others. And now they start living in an engineered culture and a mythical world, where the frustration bug will remain in their lives though the nature will be different. These little changes and varieties make them to go on. So they are constantly fighting throughout their lives to attain real happiness.

In contrast, the liberal Western culture has also its own kind of frustration standards. One can find too many smokers over here, though the advertisement of tobacco products in the media is banned. People smoke just to kill time and ease frustration and the same is the case with those addicted to drugs. The main reason of frustration is not limitation but opposite; too much liberty. It is human nature to keep wanting more as more needs are satisfied. With no restrictions, the people go for more and difficult targets, so that they can keep themselves busy. That might give them the kick and that could be adventurous in some cases since the definition of enjoyment varies from person to person. But does enjoyment mean to be carefree and selfish? Then where does the humanity factor go, and how can we introduce standards of civilization. They are too busy with themselves. Being free, they have tried everything and have gone beyond the stage of acquiring all the necessities of life. They then have to look for totally new and different things to get over their frustration. To me frustrated people are just like moaning and groaning children who, the more you keep providing them, the more they ask and are never satisfied. Should we have to look for the solution? Are we so concerned about the problem? Do we need to introduce some therapeutic ways? Are we looking for the new culture, a blend of both the Eastern and Western? A new culture that will comprise the positive qualities of both cultures. Perhaps we would be able to give people a new way to think for another half a century actively or peacefully. Perhaps we do not have to look for fabricated peace or peace plans, which now apparently the world is seeing rather than swallowing. Perhaps they will find more meaning in their lives and that would lead them to be more constructive in their approach toward life. To me life is a continuous struggle - a positive struggle for a better future.

Another aspect of both societies is the struggle of women for their rights and the contrast is quite confusing. The Western women are looking for power and command with due respect and they do not want to be treated in a discriminating way and do not want any taboos for them in the society. The overall impression is that they are being given their rights quite sufficiently but even then the contentment factor is not there. The women of the Western culture are still feeling left out and that is why they are still struggling. What do they really want to achieve? Different schools of thought have different opinions on that. On the other hand, women from the Eastern parts are very much influenced by the Western women's rights and they are fighting for the same rights which in the Western world women already have and are not happy. Now where will it lead, who will get what and how would they get their peace. In former times when people were more into religion and they practiced religious fundamentals, they were quite peaceful within themselves though small groups were always there to retaliate, but then at least a large group of people were content with their way of life. Whereas nowadays facilities and so-called rights are more in evidence then ever, even then there is more uncertainty. Why! Maybe because we spend more time and more energies in discussing religious affairs than religion itself. Since all the religions claim that they are providing a quality of life and building a positive attitude in human beings, then why can not we restrict ourselves to those golden rules and skip the controversial parts, which I believe varies in every religion. I have discussed and I have observed that the people are practicing religion no matter what, they are giving the impression that they are getting peace by practicing their religion. What could be more precious for any one than peace, since whatever we do the ultimate goal is always to get some peace. Peace is within everyone, everyone has to find it within oneself, therefore they can find their guidance with in themselves rather then to look around. It is certain by looking here and there, up and down, nobody has ever attained peace. One can only learn through their own and other people's experiences, if they are honestly explained and narrated. But the sad fact is, normally people are lying to each other, and exaggerating the facts. Well, lying could be a harsh word to use; if I adopt the Hippocratic way I could say that we explain our statements the way we like it and by doing that most of the time we forget whether we are sticking to the point or not. Naturally they would hear different comments and responses as they had predicted. I believe they have no right to blame people since they are not even serious themselves. But I am afraid these things are happening in our daily life and we are continuously suffering and keep complaining, whereas if we look into the matter we ourselves are the creators of the problem. We can very easily find the remedy if we just check ourselves.

To all the world Australia was the land of opportunity, a place where jobs were in abundance. In this haven for job-seekers, there was yet another vital attraction, it was easy to find women as well. Since Aussies do not believe in the three "W's" (women, wealth and weather), therefore ample of "W's" were available. Well, rumor has it that this is the case over there. But in part of the rumor it is said that to obtain both secure jobs and a true life-partner are not quite possible. Indeed, such are the attributes of that continent cum country.

I worked in a few organizations on temporary basis, it took me almost six months to find a job suited to my qualifications and interests. It was in one State concern, and we had to deal with all Sydney, and thus New South Wales government authorities. For the first time in my career I was part of the bureaucratic functions and I realized that the system was the same all over the world. Also, here in Australia people held the same view of the bureaucratic system as did the other parts of the world. I was not thinking on different lines either, but now, working as a part of that system I could see the other side of the picture. I wanted to work as efficiently as I could and to compel the people to positively change their approach towards the bureaucratic system. Well that was my thought since I had been given a chance to work with them and naturally I could not change the whole structure but I do believe that every body has to contribute their share at their level, so I did. By performing my duties the way I wanted, I got peace and to me that was a big recognition, though I heard many positive complements from my colleagues and superiors. I am convinced that every human has a duty to contribute their share to any society and system and as long as everyone is realizing their responsibilities then there is no need to lean on others' shoulders. It is very natural when everyone thinks that they have to do something then as a matter of fact everything is being done by someone, at the end everyone is someone and believe me nothing will be pending. Also, the staff of bureaucratic organizations are human beings too and thus are susceptible to error and omission. They certainly do justify their duties, what usually happens however is that people submitting their documents and complaints, give incomplete information and expect the staff to cover up their incompetence and trace all their records easily. I agree that the paper work is painstakingly slow, and this is often due to the slackness of the official concerned and largely due to miscommunication between the employee and the client. Often there is misinterpretation on both sides which slows the whole process of the work.

I am not being wholly defensive; I simply believe that if we give complete and accurate information to such organizations, not only would we get better outcome, but a faster response from the staff. Definitely, good management is also necessary to ensure full efficiency of these organizations. And it is a good manager who would know how to handle situations. The atmosphere of these offices is also very important, and it is the management's duty to provide friendly working conditions which would bring out the best in the work of each employee. In an atmosphere full of tension, no one would be up to the mark.

In the western offices, no one is working more then the scheduled hours for work. If they have to work for extra hours it would be for extra payment. Whereas, in most of the Eastern parts, it is considered to be very normal for the employees to work for an extra hour or so, without any extra benefits. The employer takes for granted that his employees would work longer whenever required but with no extra payments. Now people are bound to work under those conditions since their is no water tight labor law which covers the basic rights of all the laborers, and the unemployment in those countries is very high too. Therefore they are being psychologically and physically blackmailed by their own people. That is why in the Eastern world people have more hostility towards each other than in the Western world and certainly the economical issue is on the top. Here the miscommunication between the employer and employee develops. It is very logical that any extra work and time that the management takes from its workers, should be paid for, that is certainly the right of employees. But this could be in the civilized cultures, I do not mean by any means that in those countries where people are not being paid their wages honestly are uncivilized or criminal places but certainly they have a lot of catching up to do.

Both the Eastern and Western cultures are worlds apart, no doubt about that, but there is a subconscious affinity between the two societies. Unfortunately, no one from either side is willing to adopt the positive factors of the other. It is mostly the people from the Eastern side who have the opinion that it is feasible for them to adjust in the Western society. As we know people always like to copy someone who has gained something in their lives. Since the Western world is quite powerful economically as compared to the other world, that is why it is and has been always a center of attention, particularly nowadays since materialism is given the highest priority all over the world. People keep looking for their opportunities to beat each other materially they do everything they can and this appears to be normal practice. The Eastern people do the same. They mould themselves as much as they can, but in the process they loose their identities and in some cases orientation. Having lived in the liberal Western society, it is quite impossible for them to go back to what would seem to them a very conservative society with no freedom whatsoever. Statistics show that such people then, complain about their own culture. They fail to keep up relations with their families back in their homelands. Also no one can visualize and understand their situation and this creates schism between them and their families which keeps on growing. They thus, go on living in their adopted culture but get no contentment and peace.

The main victims are their children who lead unbalanced lives and forget their real roots and origin. Such children fall prey to frustration and begin to have psychological problems. I believe such parents should make a clear decision before they decide to bring a child in this world. How can you expect a child to solve all the cultural tangles which you could not solve yourself. We need to be more responsible for our actions, as long as grown ups are making decisions to choose their life style, its fair enough. But the moment innocent lives become a victim of their elders' decisions then society should be concerned since it can happen with any child or any body's child. Its always better to think before making decisions before things get out of hand.

As regards expatriates from the Western culture it is mostly women who go for the men of the Eastern side thinking them to be quite gullible and naive. The reason why Western women go for the other countries' men could be they are more adventurous than Western men. At least they have to be proud that they have beaten men in some areas of life. In the Western world self-happiness is the elixir of life. The people go for self-satisfaction irrespective of the means of attaining it. And the Western women are no exception, spending a few years of their lives quite happily. Well, that is quite evident how can people make people happy without having their own happiness. If that statement is true then they might be doing huge work for humanity, though in some cases they are doing it only for charity.

There certainly are revolutionary people in both societies who adopt the other culture and try to swim against the tide, for doing that one should have good reason for oneself and self-motivation as well. Apart from the energy which is definitely required to undertake this hard task, such couples plan mutually and adjust as much as they can to each other's culture. Their approaches are very practical and positive and they do find mental peace in some cases. It is very necessary to be open-minded in such situations, then there are good possibilities of a secure relationship and any repercussions are ultimately solved by the cosmopolitan couple. Just as a child begins school and his learning and understanding starts, so it is with the relationship of the couple; they learn from each other and have a constructive and happy life together. Also, there is a chance of misunderstandings and hatred for the other's culture. Essentially we should try to be broad-minded and always take care of the other person. We should be forgiving and not condemn people for having their own approaches towards life, even if we do not think it is right. Just think of the words "sorry" and 'excuse me' that we use freely many times a day, Do we really mean them? Are we really practicing to care for other people? If we are, we are then very healthy and considerate.

In Australia I was not happy, not due to any dislike of the society and culture, but due to my homesickness which was lingering on. My job was very important and successful, but I made the final decision to go back to Pakistan. Even though the circumstances were unhappy (my father's death), I still felt joy at going back to live in my own country.

I was very ambitious about living in my homeland, but that was to no avail. I was like a person trying to sail in two boats, which ultimately made me go out of the country again and this time I decided I would not be returning. Personally, I do not go for abrupt changes like chameleons. I do believe in random changes, but constructive and positive changes. In this age of technology, changes are occurring very fast. The most fundamental change is the attitude of the people towards the struggle for life; people now want to initiate their career with high ranking jobs, entrepreneurs now want profits right away, which is a short cut attitude. We do know there is a large number of probability that the short cut ways are not the durable ways. We might get a huge amount of profit by adopting them but certainly not in the long run. Therefore we cannot encourage this kind of attitude as the constructive way of life. One has to look for the statistics, the market strategy and consult the professionals to cover risks as much as possible. One should follow the process and the rules of the game, otherwise there is a high chance of being becoming distraught or ending up deeply depressed. Then in these kind of cases people sometimes spend their whole life but cannot recover their depression. What is the harm to think before launching the plan rather than to suffer deeply for a long period. Self-gain and materialism have become the order of the day and there is less consideration for the genuine needs. People go more and more for their own wishes and this goes for today's generation. We care for our own desires and wishes more than other people and their needs. Most of the people might think there is no harm in doing that as long as they are not disturbing others' comfort. But frankly speaking, our approach is selfish and what we do is mould the rules to our own satisfaction. Everyone has his own interpretation of the rules and naturally this is according to his own needs and wishes. We change the rules rather than accept that we are selfish. But we have to prove ourselves to be perfect, though at the same time knowing that nobody is perfect which has been proven over and over again.

Why do people have to pretend and to always keep giving explanations? Perhaps we are trying to show other people that we are superior and try to put them down to get personal satisfaction. Are we superior? Are we insecure? To me it is understandable when some one will say to you that you are wonderful or marvelous, but what I do not understand is when you will start praising yourself as we all know self praise is no recommendation. Then here comes the question, what are you trying to hide or which part of your insecurity are you trying to cover? It is the general impression that everyone wants to beat each other without knowing whether they have the talent for that. Everyone wants to prove that they are very special and whatever they are doing is extraordinary work. Do people really work because they realize it is their duty. Also do people get education just for the sake of it or for a career in which they can prove themselves and get satisfaction. In most of the cases it is a matter of survival, I would say they do not have much choice.

I have seen people working in welfare organizations who are not interested in their work but are doing it for money's sake and also to keep out of the unemployment problem. Well, it makes sense to do something, rather than to be dependent but at the same time social welfare departments of any organization do need people having at least an interest in public relations so that they can give a good impression of the organization as well as good example of humanity. We need people who are really interested in their work so that they can perform their duties happily and we can use one hundred percent potential of each individual, and then there will be less competition or blame for snatching each other's rights. Everybody might be willing to give others what they really want. Here, before going further I will explain my point of view. I will give the example of a child who is forced by someone else to give his toy to another child. First he would retaliate and finally will hand it over. Naturally, he would be very unhappy and would be hateful towards the other child to a certain extent. Then he would develop the feeling that he has been deprived of his right. On the other hand, if he had willingly given the toy to his playmate, he would be happy and satisfied. We are seeing this daily and it is happening in front of everyone of us, then why cannot we even learn from our actions. Sometimes small things can change big people's lives. Thus it is quite evident, that in society if we force people to get a job in which they have no interest or for which they have no aptitude, they will certainly not be fully productive or constructive and will ultimately grow to be victims of depression. Whereas, if we give everyone a chance to work in their own merits and interests, we will get maximum output and the result will be a constructive and healthier society.

I have observed that most of the people of both cultures avoid to take the initiative to communicate with each other. It is difficult when one seems very foreign to the other, one then feel reluctant to communicate with the other. There are so many differences in opinions, thoughts and the styles of living, particularly when one party goes to the other side to live, they have to face an already existing reputation of them. This is a very common attitude on either side; to have a permanent opinion of the expatriates from the opposite side. This is the main psychological factor in the reluctance to get to know each other. Also the person who is giving a hand has always the upper hand and same is the case with the industrial world. People from the Asian countries and East Europe go to these countries to work there and ameliorate their status in life. Mostly they amass their fortunes and return to their homeland, where they can live a better life. This is possible due to the obvious economic difference.

In some parts of the world the family values are very different i.e. in the Asian world it is not strange that only one family member is working and others are counting on that individual, and what is really amazing is that they still have a big family system like the Irish to the present day. Sometimes the head of the family does not allow other family members to work. So it is quite a peculiar situation, peculiar in the sense that they are suffering economically and they are limiting their sources as well. That is why, even working in foreign countries they have to keep supporting their families back in their own homelands. It is thus mostly due to unemployment and poor working conditions in their own countries since the inflation rate is quite high in that part of the world, that they are led to travel for better opportunities in life. Living in the industrial world such people generally however can not maintain a good standard of life since they have the responsibilities of their families back home. They are being watched with a different eye by the locals, who cannot understand their problems and occasionally they become the victims of their hostility. They then acquire the reputation that although they are earning sufficiently, they still are not maintaining good standards. Due to such misunderstanding, the local people get the impression that this is because of differences in cultures, whereas facts are entirely different. They do try to keep up with the pace of life, though it is quite hard for them. They had never practiced and they had never seen many things before they entered in this world, therefore they have to pay the penalty for lack of knowledge and awareness. That has nothing to do with the culture, it has everything to do with the technology.

We know lack of technology has made them the Second and Third world respectively. The Asian and Eastern people also think that the Western people are ignoring them just because of difference in color and creed. This is certainly very extorted thinking, but I would here state that it is definitely true in some cases. However, we should ignore and discourage such destructive and narrow-minded thinking and encourage the better side of the picture. Would we be able to find the solution in the near future? I hope we do, so that everyone can find their way and we can minimize the differences and make this world a lovely place to live.

I had heard a lot of comments about the Western people and one such statement really astonished me and forced me to think it over, some people might find it funny and some realistic. I came across this statement while I was sitting with a bunch of Africans and discussing the day to day problems. One of them come up with this idea that dark-skinned people are dark only in color, but from the inside they are clean and fair and whatever they have to say, they do expose; Whereas, the white-skinned people are black from the interior and very sneaky. Also, they are the world's greatest diplomats, showing you meaningless smiling faces, and laughing at you in private.

I tried to explain to this person that we are all human beings and have no such difference, but to no avail. Though I personally think it is quite a big statement and very direct, I have to write it other wise it will be difficult for me to portray the picture. He did not concede and it looked to me all of them had the same opinion, so I ended the discussion by telling him that perhaps he had more knowledge and awareness about white people! To me it was quite unnecessary to prolong the debate on this particular topic. I got their message very clearly, but I believe, irrespective of what culture you belong to, it is a very human and civilized gesture to keep a smiling face. It is a very positive and friendly approach to deal with people. Such behavior also depicts the patience of a person in a confused and tensed situation. I did adopt this particular way of behavior while I was interacting with them, though we had created a tense atmosphere. In this way, I gave a very friendly impression, and so do other people when they go about with cheerful and bright faces. As regards feelings, it is very difficult to analyze them, only God knows perfectly about the inner emotions and thoughts. It is very natural then, normally we are attracted to outward gestures of a person and of course we would want to meet with smiling and friendly people, irrespective of what their inner feelings are. As long as they appear satisfied and look happy that is what matters - to be happy and render other people happy.

Usually, people are quite outspoken in their opinion of others, and do not care for their feelings or what drastic effects their statements would render. It is very true that everyone thinks themselves to be a good judge and psychologist to some extent. And yes, we do have to try our best to get an idea about other people but that does not mean that we should impose our opinions and decisions on them. Freedom of thought and opinion should be there, but there should be no enforcement, that is quite contrary to civilization. Of course it is easier said than done; and the consequences are that opinions and statements begin to play a negative role in society, and it is here that cultural discrimination enters the scene. Such societies then go on to be conservative and unhealthy. Our duty is to try and curb such negative factors instead of always criticizing the others, we should analyze ourselves first.

Why can't we understand that selfishness is inherent in human nature? Therefore why can't we use our educational qualifications, standards of civilization and the golden rules of our respective religions to teach us to love and care for each other. Perhaps by sticking with our respective values we might be able to control our selfish instincts and that would be helpful for us to improve ourselves. We know there is no religion in this world which preaches to think only for oneself, the main message of all the religions is to help and care for our fellow human beings. Apart from all the controversial ties among religions, people still can find their guidance by practicing this golden rule and can make their lives happy and worthwhile for others. Naturally people can attract others more by loving them than by creating distances or hate among them that is very evident. Now we need to ask ourselves - do we really want to establish a healthy environment around us or not? Let us make it clear that there will be no miracles to let this happen! We have to think and move ourselves to make it happen. As we know even " God helps those who help themselves ". Let us accept that we are all born selfish, and the civilization of all the prevailing cultures in this world teached us how to interact with each other, and we end up by practicing what we have learned in the beginning of our lives. That is how the basic orientation of human beings develop, which is really hard to change but one can always improve oneself. Therefore it is our duty to teach our coming generation, how to love and care for others, so that we can make a good team on this planet in the coming future.

In Asia, it is the general impression that there is one culture prevailing in the Western world, since they have so many cultures around there. People immigrating to this part of the world feel that they are entering in one new culture in which they would not find any difficulty to mingle. In Europe itself there are differences in the culture; the French do not find any affinity with the English and would encourage you not to talk in English with them. On the other hand the British think themselves unique and superior to the rest of the Europeans. That is why all the European countries have most of the time unity against them, politically as well as socio-economically. Well it is hard to judge all the community but certainly one can smell some sort of prejudice among them. They can be very hostile particularly when things do not go the way they have planned. They want to be dictators irrespective whether they have talent or not. A good example of their behavioral attitude one can see even in the sports. Though sports are meant to make people healthy and positive in Football and Cricket which are two their major sports they have touched depths of ill manner.

If we statistically analyze the topmost European countries, it is France and Germany who can said to be economically superior. It is on psychological basis that the English feel themselves to be superior to the rest of their continental fellow people. They simply have to be different and think it their right to be so. Each country is trying its best to improve itself and criticize the other European countries' policies, but at the same time they are thinking on unity levels as well and they want to make all the continent stronger. Therefore they have introduced many accords among themselves, but Britain has refused to be a participant in most of them. Well, I am not a political person, therefore I am not going into any political debate as well, but I am a strong believer in unity, therefore I would say that people and the leaders of any country have a moral duty to look after their people and do some positive work for the coming time so that they can be remembered, as well as appreciated by their own people. Whereas the reality is quite different; mostly people get fed up with their leaders even during their tenure.

Since I am talking about the differences within cultures I would like to quote the Benelux Treaty; as we know this agreement is among The Netherlands, Belgium and Luxembourg. Though they are very small countries even they have a race and competition among themselves. If one is sitting in Holland it would be very normal to hear a fair amount of criticism especially about the Belgian people; like the English never spare the Irish and the Indians as soon as they get their chance. The problem is they are not criticizing, only they are eventually making judgment for all of their lives and then these thought patterns are passed on to the next generation. The Dutch are quite hostile towards the German and Belgian people. They might not like the word hostility but I am afraid it is so. The Dutch media would be a good example to quote if anyone has any doubts about this statement. It will be very normal to hear jokes about Germans and Belgians particularly on television, certainly that leaves some impact on the young generation and after a period of time these suspicions became accepted as reality, which is quite annoying. That is why the media of any country is very important. Their duty is not only to entertain the public but they have to think how to make these adverse factors vanish from their homeland, which are rotting their societies. So I believe the media people will consider my humble request some day and rather than write on sensational matters, they will find some time to write on real problems, otherwise the time is not too far when people will start hating each other.

Ex-Yugoslavia is the current example in front of us. The Iran-Iraq war and the Gulf war are the quite relevant catastrophes for our education as well, where the same cultural people have taken the rights of living from their own fellow country people. I wish these kinds of incidents will never ever happen again for the sake of mankind. But we need to work hard for the positive outcomes.

We should also concentrate on the differences within one culture and not always on the differences of two cultures. That is the reason an emigrant would find it difficult to become immersed in different cultures simultaneously. People are prepared to let go of their own culture as much as they have to, and willing to learn their new country's way of life. Apart from the other reasons due to which they have left their respective countries, the major reason is most of the time to polish and equip themselves and to learn more about other cultures as much as they can. But because there is mixture of culture within one society, that makes it hard for them to adjust quite comfortably. Also, it is quite difficult to determine the boundary line of any culture. The people then have the problem of determining their own boundaries in their new homeland. They have to decide, or rather are forced to in some cases, where they should limit their original culture and adopt their new one.

Since we know traveling and meeting people from other cultures makes people more open-minded all this is a learning process. They are learning about cultures in the world and thus more about human nature. But, we do need to enlighten the people who believe in culturalism, they need to broaden up their vision. It is culturalism which is creating a strong wall between human beings and we should, in the cause of humanity, try to break down such barriers. That does not mean people should not promote their culture or practice and preach to other generations. Of course every culture should be preserved for the forthcoming generations since it is the part of history, but we should not be rigid or biased with any other culture at the same time. There should be freedom of choice so that people can concentrate more on development work and can easily ignore the destructive factors.

HUMAN PSYCHOLOGY

THIS IS ONE OF THE most vast subjects in the world. There have been endless discussions and numerous books written on this topic. Psychologists are still trying to figure out the kinds and types of human beings. Human nature and the human brain are still being studied but still no one has come with adequate solutions to analyze the human being. One fact inherent in human nature is selfishness. I am not going into the reasons of this human factor. To me, what is important is to kill or lessen our wishes and try to think about other people and their needs for a change. I would explain further by making an analogy; when a consumer buys an item, first the seller will discuss the advantages of the item and the benefit it will give to the consumer. Most of the time it happens that people just listen and the moment they ask the price they decide not to buy that item. That does not mean they do not like the person or the item itself, the reason may be their budget does not allow them to have that item at that particular moment. The one who is selling them will not be annoyed later on by thinking that it was just waste of time. Infect the idea for both sides is positive, the consumer learned more about the product and made up his or her mind how to deal with it in future, the seller introduced the product to one more consumer. This is a routine affair between the sellers and the consumers over the commodities on sale. But in the trainings and seminars which are conducted for the sales staff, the major issue is always the method and the means of interaction with the public. In their basic training they learn how to be polite and patient.

Well, the reason I picked this example is that I just thought why can not we show such patience and logic in our life styles? We would be then more peaceful and would lessen the cultural differences as well. Suppose two persons quarrel and fight with each other, naturally there is a chance that they become bitter enemies. Now what will happen is that they will keep trying to have supremacy over each other and it will be an endless story. Whereas if one of them behaves rationally and lets that particular event be forgotten then there is a possibility the one who has forgiven will get the peace, and the other one will be always worried subconsciously. So sometimes just forgetting the bad events in life can make people more worthy. Though by taking revenge we can start a new way of life, that will lead to negativity and it will be a never-ending story and nobody will ever get peace. The choice is very clear - we need to ask ourselves what kind of future are we looking for ourselves and for our forthcoming generations. The answer is very obvious; not to encourage misbehavior in society. If someone misbehaves with us and we simply ignore that person, not only would we be playing a healthier role but we would also be discouraging misbehavior and ill- manners in society. Since a society is comprised of individuals, and each individual has a duty to be an active participant, so that every individual will be proud to contribute to the creation of an ideal society. By doing that we can make this world brighter for our children and for our future leaders.

To introduce the concept of self-confidence and individuality, I would start by saying that the people of the western culture are more self-confident and this is a very important factor of that culture. I have personally noted that the people even living on dole are self-motivated and confident of their way of life, apart from few who are really abusing the system. They do not disturb other people just because they are not getting more money for living. They are positive-minded and battle with their situations, always keeping their target in mind and know subconsciously that they will ultimately achieve their goals. They then, do not worry about their present, temporary phase of their lives.

It is with pleasure that I would cite an example here. In Sydney I was living with three more people in a house. Three of us had regular jobs with reasonable salaries, but the fourth one was on dole. Most of us were working and studying as well, therefore we had very little time for socializing. We normally saw each other on weekends and mostly our conversation started and ended with the weather. One can say we were all workaholics and had no time for so-called rubbish. But I want to write about one mate, the only one on dole. He came from a British family, but had been living in Australia for twenty-five years. He was an auto mechanic and a good artist. Painting was his hobby and I have seen many of his paintings and admired them. His weekly income was far below the minimum salary, though in those days the average minimum salary was almost Aus. $ 300. From his limited earning, he was paying rent for his room and paying all his necessary bills, including his car bills. Whatever was left he spent for his personal living including the expenses of his hobby; painting. Well it does not sound possible but believe me it was not impossible, because he was managing somehow. He was also a mechanic but had not got any official license. Occasionally, he repaired cars, which he brought from other mechanics and the funny thing is that they knew he did not have his license but at the same time they knew he was a damn good mechanic, that was why they gave him some of their work and made some money through him. They never offered him a job because he did not have the piece of paper, which would assure them that he was a recognized mechanic. That is how he was managing his life.

I have mentioned all this to explain that though this person had many problems, he never lost his self-confidence and identity. He was very lonely as anybody can imagine, I can say I have never seen such a lonely person in my entire life, but he was to me a man full of life and color. I had never seen him asking money or requesting people to buy his paintings, though he still had lots of paintings with him. I had seen them myself and they were covered with the layers of dust, showing the length of time the paintings had been untouched. But I also noticed that he really loved his work and certainly expected other people to respect his hobby and work as well. The only time he got angry was when someone devalued his hobby and art, otherwise I have never seen him quarrelling with any person. He once explained to me that now that he was in his forties and though he did not have an official license he knew his job and the bloody workshops knew about his skills as well. Then why should he have to to be downcast, if they were not employing him now, they would not offer him a job afterwards. At least that was the way he thought and that could be his fear as well. I did explain my point of view which was quite contrary in this regard but it seems he was quite stubborn in that particular issue. He was calling himself a man of principle, he had his rules and principles of life and he would not change just because of money.

I wondered why he would not work since he was such a skilled person but I did not know his convictions behind the reason for not working. What most impressed me and convinced me was his approach, the way he had created the scenario while explaining his life to me. I appreciated him and feel proud to write about him, certainly he was an intellectual. He was not a materialistic person and his approach was not sneaky. His attitude was thoroughly humble and I would certainly say that he was a gentleman. This has not been a solitary example; likewise there are many Westerners who live with the same convictions as those of my old mate. Such self-confidence in oneself and individuality are a reflex action of the Western people. It is their positive ness which makes them self-determined and brave to face the problems of life.

As regards the East Europeans and people of the Eastern cultures, their thinking and approaches are quite different from that of Western people. The East European countries and the Eastern countries are not as advanced as the First world countries and thus the people have developed a psychological attitude. It is very hard to over come the complexes. Once one gets the impression that one is lesser or better some how than others, then the downfall starts. Well, it took the Western world ages to become distinguished as the leader of the world, it is possible for the other parts of the world as well. It is always healthy to follow good examples. But the key is, they have to keep their attitude positive and promote the idea of unity among people. Then the time is not so far when all of us will be the same and there will be no so-called First, Second and Third world. I believe people are the same, if they can change the fate in one part of the world, they can do it in the other as well.

But even then if I have to make a comparison on current facts, it is quite inevitable that the Eastern people are a bit impatient in character and tend to lose their patience and nerves very quickly. If they face problems and consider obstacles as routine of life, then they might have more patience. Naturally when someone does not know what is happening around then there is a high risk of becoming impatient. People of that part should know their goals, so that they can learn how to be more content in life. This does not mean that all the Eastern people are impatient, I am talking in general terms. I would say the majority of the people are extra-conscious and some times impulsive as well. This is why, one would have noticed that the Eastern people including the East Europeans have a more irrational approach compared to the West Europeans. They are quite rational in their attitude and that is why most of the time they do consider other people and show patience. I would conclude this topic by saying that if one is organized and working within the system, one would have a remote chance of misunderstandings and having disputes with other people. On the other hand, people who think that they are the system, and think to organize the people as well as find flaws in the system, would make it pretty difficult to achieve an objective. Because we are living in a society we have to follow the rules and the regulations. We should follow the channel - how to resolve problems in the society rather than to take the law in our own hands and go beyond the limits. This would strengthen our own convictions and make us more confident and goal-oriented.

ROLE OF ELDERS

I N CULTURAL RACISM, A BIG question mark has risen about the role of people and especially the elder people. It is a natural phenomenon that children are born into the same belief system as their parents. A child born in a Muslim family would be a born Muslim and so on with the other religions. We can not blame a child for choosing the religion and thank God we are not doing that. But what really worries me a lot is why are we expecting other people to join our religion? It is human nature to dislike change. People just want to live their lives the way they have learned in the beginning. I am afraid statistics have proven that the ratio of the people who really love to explore is quite minimal. If this is true then let people practice what they want to, and let's start respecting each other's beliefs. Where is the fun in blaming and discriminating between religions, what are we getting? Bloodshed, surely nothing else. How can we attract the coming generation to the religious methodology if we keep going on like that. We need to check our behavior at this moment while we still have time, rather than blame the new generation for neglecting religious themes. We need to check ourselves now otherwise I feel no hesitation to write that we are criminals.

Another example is a well- known proverb, "A man is known by the company he keeps" and again, "Birds of a feather flock together". I will now come to the reason of citing these examples. If our elders would play a positive role in society and train and educate the children properly without any notion of racism and discrimination, it would then be possible to introduce a good system in society. How are we going to do this and whose duty is it? It is everyone's duty in the sense that we should keep a check on ourselves. If every person starts thinking about his or her role in society and justifies it, then that would make way for a better society and would make it easy to maintain that standard of society. Whereas our approach is to try to always save ourselves by giving excuses, and the person in the wrong would always be pleading. Why do we need to plead? I think the moment one thinks that one has done something beyond the norms of society then one feels the need to clarify one's position. This is the normal behavior in society.

The question is what is normal? And what is abnormal? Like people cleaning their noses in public and in office meetings. Is that normal or is it abnormal? Such a gesture is sometimes a great disturbance for the other people present, especially in the library when the people are concentrating on their work. This is a normal habit in society but no one is taking the responsibility of denouncing this habit by telling youngsters and other people as well. I do not blame youngsters when I see them squashing their noses publically and rather very comfortably, since they do not feel that they are doing anything strange and weird. Nobody perhaps taught them, but this habit annoys lots of people. This is what I mean by saying that if we teach our children properly from the beginning, then those children would grow up as responsible human beings and play their role in society and that would make a more neat and clean living atmosphere around us. Everyone would then follow the positive rules in the society made by responsible people. When I am using the word responsible I mean those people who are elected by the society to be representative for them. The people who really work hard for the cause of society and follow a positive pattern of life. Can we think on these lines? Certainly we can solve our problems by ourselves and rather than to criticize others, we should evaluate ourselves first. When we start appreciating other people, we would certainly be more broad- minded and then we would overthrow the negative aspects of society.

In this context if I compare the people around thirty to thirty-five years of age and the older people above fifty years, then I would say that the younger people are more polite and open-hearted. That is not to say that the elders are impolite, but they are comparatively more conservative. This would be due to the age factor and what they have learned from their superiors. Most of the time they keep practicing what they have learned, though sometimes things do not make sense for them either. But they keep practicing, perhaps they are afraid of experiencing new things. What I never understood is though people have adopted their ways of life, they do not know the logic behind that, and are even confused about their own convictions. Then the question springs to mind: what is the fun of living? One has to live one's life only one time then why not live happily and why can not people clarify their confusion by sharing with each other rather than to keep compiling and then transferring to the other generation. We have to be at least honest in this aspect that whatever we are getting in this world in an improved form, someone had worked hard to attain that for us at some stage. Now we are the beneficiaries of someone else's work and that feeling gives us the kick that we have to keep thinking on the positives changes for our coming generations.

Changes are now occurring very fast in the society. Today's youth do need changes, the changes which will minimize their frustration and give them an opportunity to think more on constructive projects. To me it seems quite the right approach to this prevailing situation. If the changes are good it makes a person to be on the move and when the things are moving then one has to be always alert. Being alert, one is using ones positive energies and the more energy one will use the more fresh energies one will get, since that is how the human body works. There are changes that are occurring automatically without the intention of the people and are producing positive results. If our intentions are such - that we want to change the system for the better - then the result would probably be most positive. And we will find our base as we are striving to do.

HUMAN WISHES

HUMAN WISHES ARE UNLIMITED AND to calculate and to specify them would not be an easy task. But it is a very important part of any one's life, it shows the characteristics of the person. To be goal-oriented and to have a wish are two different things. It is quite evident that high hopes and wishes bring lots of happiness in many people's lives. Our wishes play a very fundamental role in life. How do wishes play such an important role in our lives and how can we control or put a limit to our wishes? It is very interesting; no one likes to be under any limit, as we know there are many limits in everyone's life. That is why people are even more reluctant while they are making their wishes and they do not want to put any limit. This word reflects a boundary wall for their freedom of doing or not doing anything. Wishes are mostly beyond reach, that is why they are wishes. Otherwise they can be realities - and by the time we succeed in fulfilling our last wishes and desires, we have already made our minds for the new ones. So the process goes on, we can say it is a never - ending story.

Naturally we get frustrated sometimes because of our high wishes, and end up by paying the high price of our life. I would like to mention here how we build high hopes and wishes even within our close relationships, and how dearly this can cost us. While I refer to it as a mistake I must say as soon as one begins to have expectations from a relationship one ruins it. During my travels I met many people from different cultures, some of them inspired me and left an impression on me. It is one of the reasons that I have compiled all the events. Well, I have to stick with the topic. I have seen well-matched and happy couples who are unable to obtain all their wishes and desires, as is the case in everyone's life. They start disagreeing with each other and ultimately end up divorced. Later on they realize their mistakes and each one feels that he or she was at fault, but none of them takes the initiative to confess that they were at fault. The moment they have got the final result none of them is really happy because I have never seen many people who can digest the "D" word easily. No couple has an ultimate wish to get acquaintance with the "D" word. But now the situation is too far gone and they have very little chance left, to make everything over once again.

It is good to have ambitions and wishes as long as they are not suffocating one's life. Without inner joy there is no pleasure in anything. Stubborn attitudes can sometimes destroy the beauty of life. It is quite painful to see that the divorce rate in the Western world is far higher than in the Eastern world. The reason could be more liberty and free society. If freedom is disturbing our way of civilization then certainly we need to check ourselves. Since the word freedom sounds very positive itself, the result automatically should be positive, but I am afraid the results are the other way around in many cases nowadays, particularly in the free part of the world. Though Eastern people have to learn a lot from the Western world but certainly not in this particular area. Eastern values are quite powerful and they need to be more strengthened rather than destroyed. If they do destroy their values, soon they will invite yet another trouble into their society.

Talking about high ambitions, I have given an example about married life - why, because this is a very important issue today when the number of the divorces are touching the sky. I never understand why people get married in the first place when they have no such commitment between them. What is the fun to marry for a short period? Are people marrying only to get the title? To me to marry someone is a life-time commitment, it shows people's personalities. Because no one can make standards of commitment in one day, it is actually a process which people have learned from their own experiences. If one cannot honor one's major commitment in life then what can one expect in future, apart from the exceptional cases.

What usually happens is that everyone has ideals about married life. When a couple marry and start their practical life together, they both want to follow the ideals and style of living that they had determined. Naturally two people living together would have their own way of thinking and living. It is very natural that one would want to lead the other partner. Every person would want the command in this field - be it a laborer or a king. It is a matter of winning and losing even in our married lives though most of us do not believe this, but does denial rectify the problem? No certainly not. We know that when two groups are at war, one would be the winner and the other would be the loser. Once one group will win the war, then the loser has many problems to face for freedom. In another situation one group would denounce war and go for peace. That could be hard for any one group to denounce, but certainly by taking this action both groups can find their own peace for the moment and could do so for the future as well. Would not that be the best solution for this problem? In this way we might always get solutions. When both persons want to lead each other, one would win and other would lose, or else they can both adjust to each other. But since such things are easier said than done, the couple would want to have command over each other.

Another problem is that mostly we do not consider our faults and go on making mistakes. Then a certain situation comes when we reach the point of no return, if we want to come back either we have to do a lot to cover our deficits or we have to pay a huge amount of penalties. But we still feel it an insult to follow rules and regulations, since most of us believe that they are stereo-types. We have a prestige problem in these matters. We are from birth status-conscious, some accept it and some do not. For some it takes less time to understand and for other it takes quite a long time to understand reality. These factors are also a cause of divorces, we go on thinking about ourselves, our egos and prestige but not of the other person. I sincerely hope that we will start giving more respect and admiration to other people. Just like when we put more sugar in our tea to make it more sweet; in the same way respecting other people would make them respect us. We will get the same reaction as Newton's law of motion states; "Every action has the same and opposite reaction". Also, there is the very apt proverb, " Do unto others as you want others to do unto you".

We would thus be giving and equally gaining respect. When two people sharing life together start respecting each other and their wishes, then there is no way that they would not achieve their goals or targets. They would certainly be more successful and peaceful in life and it will give the feeling of being more complete. As most of my religious friends believe when a man and woman are living happily together they can produce anything what the world wants from them. Is it a truth or a myth? We can not decide until unless we honestly work for our relationships but the figures show a completely different picture. Surely we need to be very honest in our relationships, then we will be in the situation to move on further. In this way we can control the negative things existing in the society. Now, how to respect others and evaluate them is not a difficult question. It is quite simple. We should respect and deal with others in the same way that we want to be respected. That is the solution to this problem and it would make us all happier and more civilized. We would be respecting the wishes of other people and vice versa.

WITHIN CULTURE INEQUITY

I AM COMPARING THE EASTERN AND Western culture on the basis of discrimination and I now want to delve into discrimination within the culture. Both the cultures are heavily involved in this morbid reality. The Asians are more deeply involved than the Europeans. Belief in class system is still a very basic part of the Eastern society. The more assets someone has the more powerful and proud one feels. Naturally someone rich in any part of the world will have more resources than other people who do not have that much. But over there the story is quite different, everybody would like to be a big gun, by one way or another. By this I mean they are almost behaving as gods or goddesses in certain territories and for particular classes, and the feeling gives them a kick. and they keep passing these so-called values to their next generations. That is why we still have feudalism, tribalism and capitalism in excess in those countries.

The exciting thing is that most countries claim that they are democratic. So I think, maybe the definition of democracy varies from one part to another. People who introduce themselves as big guns are more high up in the society, and they show off their material aspects, not their talents. Also, they are trying to maintain that there should be different ways to behave and approach the different classes of the society. Sometimes it sounds very English to me, it looks like the English have some subconscious influence on them. This shows psychologically how complexed they are and their doubt in their abilities. Are they finding some excuses for themselves? Or as the saying goes ' A drowning man clutches at straw', are these people seeking for help? Usually they feel relaxed and correct to introduce their false images - false because they go for materialism rather than their true abilities and talents.

The interesting thing is that they are living the way they have chosen but still they are not happy and content. They are always at war among themselves and if in some cases they are not at war that means they have no choice. It is not that they do not want it, its only because of some reason that they have to cool themselves. During all this process lots and lots of people have to sacrifice their lives and nobody ever explained to the families why they have lost their loved ones. Everyone has their own way to explain the story. I would say it is even worse than any viral disease and there have been many debates on this issue, but the big question is who is going to bell the cat? No effective remedies are being taken to end this so-called bureaucratic system. Bureaucracy is very strong in the Eastern countries and if the same pattern of society continues, it will be an enormous task to wipe off this disease and clear the minds of the people. I would not be surprised if world faces another human virus in the very near future. It is the duty of all the world to intervene, so that we can save ourselves from another disaster. We have to be aware that it is everyone's problem and it is not just existing in one part of the world. Today it is over here, tomorrow it will be over there.

In the Western culture there is an overwhelming impression that there is no class system and no discrimination. This is the idea created by the books and the media, but is this a true impression? Is everything narrated in the books correct? Does the media always cover all the facts? It is a tricky one to answer. I have never seen any event being covered by the media with 100% accuracy. The news media is not hundred percent error proof, sometimes they make mistakes and sometimes they want to make mistakes. It is very hard for the average person to understand the reality. Therefore the existing picture is always different. That is really strange and pitiful, we need to improve our mass communication and the trends in journalism. Sensational stuff is good so long it does not change the theme of the story. For example; if they want to communicate a message" stop, do not let it go", I will not be surprised that people will get this message as; "do not stop, let it go". It is necessary that whatever we read should be fact, whereas it is not happening. It is the media which brings people either close or apart.

I have personally seen discrimination occurring in the office get-togethers, private parties and public clubs. The bosses of the companies are introducing policies to implement equal rights for all the employees, so that they can prove how generous they are in their approach toward the employees. In fact in the office meetings one can clearly observe that everyone is interacting at par, though they would be polite enough in some cases to say 'hi' to some other recognized faces. Even the big boss of the company will chat and hang around most of the time with the immediate management. It seems very normal to me and so to others in the Western world. But the Westerners do not believe in discrimination. I personally agree with it, yes, they do not believe in that discrimination which exists in the Eastern world. Since in most of the Eastern parts bosses even do not bother to mix up with the other staff, therefore they love to arrange separate parties. In some cases when they are in very generous moods they arrange small parties for the other staff as well. That is the reason which forces me to write that even the discrimination of the Western world is different from the Eastern world. Now who needs what, let them decide for themselves.

There is thus classification, and that is the psychological treatment of the employer. The people are reluctant to mix up though they are colleagues and know each other quite well. They are not supposed to believe in classification, but this fact is observed from their behavior with each other. Certainly, the Europeans do live in classification, though the class system is less obvious than in Eastern culture. The Western people are great diplomats, since they do everything behind the scenes. But the fact that there is a cover over their activities does lessen this negative factor as compared to the Eastern society. We better start thinking about this aspect very seriously since to me it is even worse than an epidemic. It is a natural fact that we need prevention against any epidemic to prevent people from more suffering. In the same way it is vital to take precautionary measures against discrimination so that we can save our societies from being corroded; and then we can play an active role against this bane of society and produce a healthy and peaceful society where equality prevails.

BEHAVIOURAL APPROACH

WITH REGARD TO HUMAN BEHAVIOR there can be no discrimination on the basis of cultural racism. Every human being always wants to adjust to the given environment and culture. The environment for any person can be positive or negative irrespective of which culture one belongs to. In Europe, the impression of the immigrants is that they are the ones involved in lawless activities and are promoting corruption. That is why corruption rate is getting higher and higher day by day in the Western part of the world.

That is the general impression of the people from East Europe and the Far East. Due to these illegal activities the Government is entitled to stop such immigrations and lots and lots of people are suffering. Even the genuine people can not travel to the Western world. In the Eastern world people can not make their holiday plans freely simply because they have to face too many restrictions to qualify even for simple holiday visits and that is developing hostility towards the Western world. Is it a reality or is it purely an allegation that due to the Eastern people crime rate has increased? Is it a better solution - to simply close eyes to such problems and get the easy way out. Hard work and understanding are required to cope with any given situations.

The important point here is that a person belonging to any culture will find it difficult to settle down in a new and strange place and environment. The basic necessities of life - food and shelter will be hard to obtain, and any person will be striving hard to achieve the solution of the immediate problems. In these type of situations, the true type or character of a person can not be judged since it would be difficult to analyze whether the person is justified or not. Here, the evil-minded person would find different ways to cheat and solve the problems. A few years ago, while I was living in Lahore where I was born and spent all my childhood, I was taking my daily after - dinner walk. It was about 11:00 pm and there was quite some hustle and bustle since it was eve to Eid-ul-Fitr, one of the festival days of the Muslims, celebrated after the month of Ramadan. The jubilation is almost like Christmas eve. While walking I usually analyze my whole day and make plans for the coming day, and I was in the middle of forming one, when I was interrupted by a young bloke about eighteen years of age who politely excused himself first and then asked for money, explaining his situation quite innocently. At first, I was very surprised to be thus interrupted, but then I believed him and thought him to be a deserving person. His appearance did not show that he was not deserving. I can very well imagine how difficult it is for anyone to ask for money and particularly from a stranger makes it more difficult. I gave him the bus fare and after thanking me nicely, he went on his way.

I continued my habitual walk and thanked God that I was not in his shoes. After about twenty minutes, I was again surprised to see the same boy asking money from other people. I got really perturbed and started wondering if he was gathering money for the next day or was he a modern beggar? I cannot even now be sure. I have my suspicions that he was gathering money for the next day, so that he could go out with his friends and enjoy himself. But the way he had adopted was terrible. Now in future if I should come across the same situation I might not react the same way I did with him, which I believe is not fair. Sometimes only one event or action can change attitudes of people's lives. I quoted this example to show how difficult it is to judge who is really deserving and who is simply cheating. This is a major reason why people are reluctant to help.

I would here quote another example. In Delft (Holland) I met one Romanian guy who was a thief and he acknowledged this fact and this I believe was his redeeming quality. That stealing is bad is besides the point I am citing here. He agreed that he was doing wrong but maintained that he was stealing to fulfill his basic necessities of life. He was about twenty years of age and a mechanic in electronics, but being a political refugee he could not work. He was given twenty guilders per week but he could not get all his basic requirements from the twenty guilders and therefore he had turned to committing theft.

He had fled from Romania because he was against the regime and could not achieve his basic human rights over there. He had therefore come to Holland in hope of earning money, naturally, but was again facing the same survival problem. His young shoulders could not bear this harsh reality. I did not know what to say to him. If I told him that I did not approve of his stealing, I would then have to give him an alternate solution rather than to simply tell him that what he was doing was bad and to force him to stop. I would only give him the substitute of working illegally which is very common. He was not allowed to work legally and he was anxiously waiting for the decision to work. But this advice was not a positive suggestion as well. And to me any lawless activities are simply illegal and bad, whether the gain is fifty guilders or hundred and fifty guilders. Most of the people will say, this is not that bad or this is less bad, but what I believe is just like an example of a pregnant woman. If you ask any woman are you pregnant? The answer would be yes or no. There is no other answer like 'sort of ' or any other. So, to me crime is crime and the nature does not matter.

In both these examples, the two persons are teenagers and in this age we really need to guide them with tact rather than by force. It is due to force or negative response from the elders that young people are prone to escapism and negative values. We need to give proper alternatives to our juniors and dependents. The young people watch their elders striving hard to achieve financial gains but failing. They keenly watch the environment around them and see their elders not achieving their goals in life. This becomes a challenge to them and they start finding short-cuts to achieve their targets. To follow any target one has to follow the system and that takes time and a lot of hard work. The young people, having seen their elders spending all their lives working hard but not achieving their ambitions, tend to cross the boundaries of law to achieve their own ambitions. The important thing for them is to get money and succeed where their elders failed.

Where money is concerned we know that wants can never be satisfied. Be it a laborer or a millionaire, they always go for more and are never satisfied. Also there is a lot of attraction in evil activities rather than the good proper channels, simply because one gets the short-cut way in the evil side. As the saying goes, "an empty mind is the devil's workshop", we need to look into this matter and need to build a strong structure so that we can control even those people who get off the track rather than to promote this frustration in the young generation. We need not to leave things alone by just saying 'it will be alright'. Nothing will be alright until unless someone will work for it. Sometimes to compensate for casual behavior one has to pay extraordinary amount.

PRETENDING UNSELFISHNESS

I HAVE ALREADY TOUCHED ON THE topic of selfishness and here I feel the need to elaborate more with emphasis on the fact that we always pretend not to be selfish. I would explain it by giving an example; I was in the main market of Delft, an old Dutch city where all sorts of multinational people can be seen. Delft has a technical university of international fame where there are many students from different parts of the world. That makes the city more attractive for the tourists. Tourists usually have knowledge of various cultures and come up with accurate opinions sometimes. One such incident occurred with me while I was visiting one antique shop in Delft. Someone introduced himself to me and at first I thought him to be some junkie asking for money since it is very normal to find such people in the busy tourist places of Amsterdam and Delft. Because I have experienced visiting other tourist places as well, therefore I normally react with very cold vibrations in the beginning. I reckon that is quite an effective way, particularly when someone is not at ease with the situation.

The person I had mentioned was in his mid-fifties and after saying hello back to him, he started talking with me. He could clearly see that I was from the sub-continent, therefore he started talking about the Hindustanis. I was very astonished to hear the word Hindustanis from him, normally people from the Western world will use the word Indians. Another surprising factor was his correct pronunciation which made me curious to know about him. To my query of his nationality, he replied that since he had traveled all the world, he felt that all the world was his, so he was a man of the world. I really liked the answer and I would say he really inspired me and I now had my full attention on him. Perhaps he thought I was an Indian, and I do not know what he thought of my response to him. He started talking about the Pakistan-India war and explained to me about Bangladesh and the Kashmir problem. He also talked about the religious conflicts between the Hindus and Sikhs. He went on to discuss the world wars in general and rounded off his discussion with the Gulf war. He certainly had ample knowledge of the world religions - Islam, Christianity and Hinduism. He had studied both the Holy Quran and Holy Bible in detail and the result of all his studies and knowledge was that he was a man full of peace. His words were to me a book full of knowledge and his message to the world was that all human beings are equal and that war was not the solution to all our problems. With war, perhaps one problem could be solved, but at the same time more problems are created for humanity and this can be seen clearly from the recent Gulf war. We should come with peaceful solutions for our problems but this in itself is a large topic and not my topic at this particular moment. I would conclude here by saying that we do have other solutions rather than war. The Gulf war was a matter of stubbornness from both sides and also a matter of false prestige. Although Kuwait is free now the losses are still there and it will take a lot of time to heal them; and yet the same policies of both Saddam Hussein and George Bush still exists and so does the probability of war.

Both these men claim to be quite religious and to think about the people - how to keep their rights and identities. They are certainly not sincere with themselves or with the people they claim to look after. We know that power is with the people, but no one wants to works as a group. People want their own palaces with strong boundaries to keep away intruders since the belief in privacy is getting stronger and stronger. The rulers of any country are indeed misusing the people in a very polished and sophisticated way. But no one in this fast and busy world has time to think on these matters. People are busy with their personal problems of getting work, finances and an established life. How can any one think collectively when one does not have food or basic necessities of life to live? That is the big reason why people are being psychologically and morally abused by their own so-called leaders. I believe they should be aware that the real power is in their hands and they should be united without being prejudiced in religion, color and culture. This was the important message I got from the man I had met and I am really proud of him and his approach towards life and humanity.

I am ashamed of myself at the way I had initially underestimated this great person. I do believe that presentation counts but I would say that facts and figures are more real. That is why I believe realities are always different than the way they are presented. I really hope that everyone would start thinking the same way as my old but wise buddy does, and then the day will be very near when we all will start loving each other, irrespective of material aspects. Here, I would like to explain the situation from another angle, when one interviewee got my full attention while I was interviewing for a company I was working with. I questioned the person about his expected salary and was greatly impressed by his answer - that, the amount of salary was not important to him; what was important for him was to achieve his target which he had made while he was still studying at university. He did not want to forfeit his goal for money. He simply wanted to work through to his goal. Certainly when he would achieve his goal, that of working on management cadre, he would automatically have a good salary. I really liked him because he was not negotiating the material but his mission, though he was getting both. So if one is sincere with one's goals and convictions of life, then one can get maximum benefit from life. But if one shows greed, one can never be satisfied or be at peace with oneself.

His answer was quite diplomatic and it sounds like 'killing two birds with one stone' but still he was a promising young man full of positive energies and I still believe he meant well too. It is quite evident that if one is sincere with oneself and with others as well, then we can have solutions to our questions and problems. Our personal intentions should clearly be defined, that helps us most of the time and others as well and we should not be scared to discuss the facts the way we want to.

ANOTHER ANGLE OF PREJUDICE

NOT MANY PEOPLE WOULD GIVE importance to this issue, but I would stress that it is small issues which give rise to the big ones. Each drop of water is important in forming a river. I want to depict how discrimination takes place in every small possible way.

I was once sitting with a few of my European friends on the beach and we were relaxing and chatting. I personally do not like the European beaches apart from the southern parts. I have seen a lot of clear blue gleaming water around the Far East and Australia. Therefore I am afraid I can not find much in Dutch beaches. People were passing us and one man stood out because of a slogan written on his T-shirt. The words were 'Cool as fuck'. This was not shocking for me since I had seen far more atrocious slogans and the Western world is very well known for its liberty. I have already discussed the subject of liberty earlier and I will pick it up later on. My other mates had also seen this gentleman. I will call him that, and one of them said, 'Oh, look at the Blackman'. I did not like his gesture of pointing and his words, and politely told him so. I have never been a person to remain silent especially when I am confused over something. I asked him why he could not simply say, 'that man'? He replied that it was not normal to wear such slogans over there and that was the reason of specifically pointing out the person. A statement which I never can understand and believe and neither do other people. We had a long debate over this with all the others participating in this controversial discussion. None of us could be convinced by each other's arguments and our debate ended in a draw. That was quite something, normally we convinced each other or we found a middle way out. But particularly on this issue everyone adhered to his or her point of view. We tried our best to change the topic and find another topic of conversation. As everyone knows it is always better to have nice discussions in a relaxing environment and for us that beach was a lovely spot on that particular day.

Now what happened next was that we saw a few white-skinned boys wearing T- shirts with the same slogan; and this showed my opponent's arguments to be lame. He started giving excuses, I finally ended the discussion by saying that we should never give strong statements about any culture particularly when we have little knowledge of that culture. Furthermore I would say even if one black person is wearing that T-shirt it does not say that every black likes it. What has that to do with his culture and background? Certainly one can judge people due to their culture and society but definitely not in this aspect. Actually they are just a few small things which can make the difference. If my friend would have said that I did not like the slogan then the situation would be very different and so would the consequences. That is why I would say the 'penny wise pound foolish' theory works.

This brings us to another question which is quite confusing for everyone - what is the definition of normality and what is not normal? Especially when we talk about human liberty, are there any limits to it? In the European culture, human liberty is the way of life there and to criticize it would bring the wrath of the people on the critic. One strong plea which always comes to my mind regarding this subject is that are we human beings or are we animals? Yes, biologically human beings are in the category of animals but according to the civilization standards which of course human beings have made themselves, we are better animals than the other animals. We have taken liberty to soaring heights and the traditional human values have been turned upside-down.

Coming back to my friend's statement of normality, I can understand his point of view, since he was brought up in the European culture and had been living there for thirty years. For him whatever he has seen all those years in his surroundings is normal and that is the way how it works in the world. Therefore no one is to blame. This behavior brought two questions to my mind - whether he really believed in racism or he did not like this level of liberty. But then I get confused here again because in the beach environment nakedness is very normal in the Western culture as well as different other parts of the world. If there is no harm to be naked then there should not be a problem about the by-product. I still believe that the consumer is normally attracted to the finished goods and is generally least concerned even about the processing. If the people, Western and Eastern are really that liberal and have no time for immaterial things, then why do they spend their precious time on discrimination and hurt other people's feelings? That is definitely not the way of civilization by any means. We are certainly far better than animals, though we can always pick some good habits from them. But once again that is purely human since human beings want to explore more and more and it is not that we do not know, it is simply the fact that no one has ever touched this matter. I am sure very soon we will recover our recoveries.

What we need is to seriously think on this problem of society and educate the people. It should be the duty of the ministry of education to provide neutral books on this topic and to solve this increasing problem in society. The time is now when there can be some control over this important issue. Otherwise it would be too late to handle this problem in any culture. Naturally the media of every respective culture should back-up this policy. As the saying goes, 'nip the evil in the bud', discrimination should be controlled and stopped now, and that can only be done by educating people.

OTHER WAYS OF CLASSIFICATION

A s I AM DISCUSSING ABOUT culture and people's approach and reaction towards different cultures, I have had the privilege of interacting with different sorts of people from various cultures and have observed them in detail. Among them are both the West and East Europeans. I got the opportunity to live with the East Europeans for a few months. When I talk about East Europeans, I mean people from Russia, Romania, ex-Yugoslavia, Poland etc. I have interacted with these people while I was living in different places and have observed them very closely. Though I strongly believe when people are living outside their countries they are quite a different people than the way they have lived their lives in their own respective places. On the other hand, it is always fun to watch the other side of the human being. That is another proof that we are living in this world with different standards, irrespective of the color, religion and the part of the world we belong to.

One of the main characteristics in the East Europeans I have observed is that they are quite restless. It is money and materials which makes them most happy. Money of course, plays a very vital role in every culture and all over the world, and there are endless disputes over it. But in the case of these people, money is extra special. In one way it is understandable since they have not seen much freedom of spending in their lives, that might attract them more towards money than any other person. It is a purely psychological effect. But that does not mean that in the other parts of the world people are not keen to earn money, certainly yes! But perhaps their way of showing it is quite different from the people who think simply and solely of money. Quoting one friend, who was an Aeronautical engineer, his one day salary was equivalent to one guilder. I was really astonished to hear this and I started to understand why money was so important for the East Europeans. If the qualified people are earning that low then what will happen to the others. He had come here to earn enough money to make him financially secure, and then he would go back to his country. He also talked against the politics and system of communism in his country. But in spite of these conditions he wanted to go back after fulfilling his financial goals, for he knew that he could only be peaceful living in his own country.

Most of the people coming for economical reasons to the Western world think along those lines because most of them do not like to quit their family and cultural ties forever. It sounds quite human, definitely it is not easy to forget family and the place of birth for ones whole life. People can change on a temporarily basis but certainly they can not change their orientation and it is against the law of nature. Rather than to discourage them and discriminate against them it is our moral duty to help those who help themselves and try to improve their life for their families. It is a very positive gesture if one will look from this angle. I really call them hero's, because they are sacrificing their lives only to protect their next generations. They are contributing their contribution the way they believe is right. Since I believe it is very hard to live in a strange world and with strangers, no one really wants to cope with such a situation and if someone is coping then it could be the case that one could not find other constructive ways according to one's own standards and vision.

These people are Europeans too, but the difference in the language and character-wise their quick reflexes show them to be different from the West Europeans. They have the same color and features, but Eastern habits tend to be aggressive. To be aggressive is not a negative quality, but certainly excess of everything is bad. To have some aggression and to be aggressive makes a lot of difference, that is why mostly people encourage assertive behavior.

Once, I was in a party where most of the other guests were East Europeans. They started explaining their culture to me. They did not know how keenly I was listening and observing them. They were talking about relationships and comparing with the Western world. They told me that they are quite different from the Western men in the sense that they take good care of their women. Whereas the Westerners have no respect for their girl-friends or even wives and they are very materialistic in their relationships. Personally, I have not seen anything distinguishing in them either, but I do respect their opinion since everyone has a right to explain one's point of view.

What I got from their conversation was that they took rather too much care. In the man-woman relationship, they saw no hesitation in killing their opponents simply for their integrity. It shows that women for them are a symbol of their integrity. That sounds very positive and fair enough. But if they force any human being to be with them and do not fulfill the basic emotional and human rights then this seems to me a tribal area life but I could not tell them so directly. By any means love can not be bought by force. I did make them feel that I did not agree with their system. They believed very strongly in the different social rights of men and women. To my earlier statement I was told that, then I would like my wife to go with another man. Now, this was a very personal question but I did answer by saying that I was not yet committed to anyone. I smiled and concluded the discussion rationally.

My argument was why are we men so rigid and conservative about the women issue. Why is there no check on men as well? In other words, a man can go for other women while a woman cannot, and the feeling and emotions of women do not matter. When a man is exposed with his manly stuff, he will be a real "MAN", but if a woman is having friendships then she is not worth it. For heaven's sake we have to get rid of this self- fabricated ideology and give fresh air to everyone, who live in this lonely planet. I do believe in double-standards but not to that extent. I knew that a few of the men sitting besides me were married, but had temporarily taken off their marriage rings since they wanted to have " some more fun ".

The next important part of the discussion was the marriage system. They do not believe in inter-racial marriages. To them, marriage between a black person and a white person was not acceptable and they thought such a marriage to be quite bad. I quietly asked the reason for such a strong belief and the person innocently replied that, then the child born out of this wedlock would be brown in color and that was not good. I use the word innocently deliberately, since the statement does not make any sense to me. Being a positive person whenever I have heard such statements in my life I never react, I simply believe that such people do not know more than that. That is how I control my anger in complicated situations.

I was now more curious than ever and probed more. They were really very serious in their point of view on marriage. I told them that I knew a very good family who were a mixture of black and white. The elders of the family had married with black people and now the family was a colored one. The children were nicely tanned and quite good-looking. But this example was put down by the others and they did not believe such a family to be good. But at the same time they did not have any valid or authentic point which made me think about their views. I decided to withdraw from the discussion and my thoughts turned towards racism. I thought for a moment that maybe they strongly believed in racism. I could not say to them the word racist, maybe they did not want to hear the word racist but certainly they have all the symptoms which lead towards racism.

One important thing I would say here, the communism we read about and study from books is quite different from what I have seen in reality. Initially I was in favor of communism but having seen it practically, I am losing my confidence in it. It seems to me just like the case of religions - in the books they are all very attractive and appealing but practically very few people actually practice it word by word as should be the case. This is one of the main reason why people are going astray from their religions. I think the same is happening with communism and this is also why people are now fleeing from it. The people in authority are manipulating the system and modifying it according to their own interests. This is the major cause of the downfall of communism.

It is just like what the priests of the different religions do. They have full power and are using it to play with the people all over the world. In fact this is the basis of segregation of people into groups who are now against each other. In other words, we are condemning other human beings by showing that we are the greatest and most true people on earth and the others are totally wrong and stupid to some extent. I have seen people strongly criticizing other groups and religions. The priests, whom everyone looks up to, should teach the people not to be critical of other beliefs, but with their practical approach attract them. We do see that there are many religious people who practice all the good points of all religions and thus show their respect for every religion. We must be sure that if we think ourselves to be the best, are we must ask ourselves if we are indirectly condemning all the other people who have a different belief from us and are we saying in a very polished way that they are dummies? Who would like to be called a dummy? Certainly and surely not even a single person on earth. This is surely against all codes of humanity and the basic rules of any religion. In conclusion I would say that we should be more practical in our actions so that we can then easily convince other people.

ROLE OF BUREAUCRACY

To TAKE CARE OF THE orphans and the children who have no other guardians becomes quite a problem all over the world. Therefore there should not be any sort of difference in the classification of children and all of them should be treated equally. It is the right of children to be given proper care and attention. It is only possible when we fulfill all the needs of a child, then we can make them good human beings with admirable qualities, as we desire them to be. We should never ever let ourselves to be affected by the color of any child. We have to make sure that every child in this world is getting the same treatment from us. People can raise the question on how to treat all the world's children in the same way. This appears to be a argument, but as a reality it is only an argument. The reality is, if all of us, no matter where and in which part of the world we live, started feeling that we need to take care of the child on the same merit, then believe me psychologically we will solve the major part of the problem. It is by being aware of and acknowledging any major issue that we can find a solution.

Scientists have made a thorough study of the nature of children and their behavioral attitude. They have speculated that the environment affects the child the most, therefore the environment is of utmost importance in the up-bringing of every child, especially in the first five to ten years of the child's life. If one looks at a child's life from all possible aspects and point of views, one will see that it is the environment and ambience of the first years which is most fundamental. Therefore for God's sake we do not have to be choosey about the adoption of any child. We can make every child a good human being irrespective of the color and the race of the child.

The topic I want to revise here is the adoption of a child, which is getting more important day by day. When I mention children, I refer to the children from all over the world regardless of the color of their skin. Now the important issue is, who's going to adopt them and how? The government of every country should desperately look for the help in this quarter, and through the media, this problem should be publicized so that the public could be made aware of this growing problem. The bureaucracy of the different countries should not handle this issue in the bureaucratic way. This problem should be solved with the help of the people. I am certain without public consent no bureaucracy can solve this growing problem in the entire world.

They should not concentrate on adoption problems regarding the color of the child. The classification of black children from white children should not be the issue and should not be discussed. They have to see and feel the nature of the problem rather than to look only at one side of the picture. Yes, from the statistical point of view, it is evident that black children have a lot more problems of adoption than the children of another skin color. It is certainly a sad fact, but it is the bureaucracy that is initiating such discrimination children. Since this is a fact of life, however sad, I have no hesitation in writing it. Should they have to publicize this matter or they have to handle it themselves? Do they have to let the public know that they can not manage without their help? These questions need to be answered by the authorities of the countries involved. There are certain rules in the bureaucratic system of which all societies are aware and an effective approach to this particular problem might be to adopt the common policy of first come first served. Certainly by adapting this policy, there would be far less trouble in handling the situation of child-adoption by any bureaucracy.

The people who go for child-adoption are fully aware of humanitarian values. The fact is one has to have great human values even to think of any other human particularly in this existing materialistic world. Surely the most important factor for the people who want to adopt a child is that there exists human being wanting to be loved and cared for, irrespective of color, religion and culture. Certainly then, one should look beyond these factors. A child, as such, has no identity; it is the parents that give the child the name, religion and culture. So, I would most certainly say that the government of some countries should change some policies on child-adoption to facilitate easier adoption and should use the media to promote child-adoption, rather than to promote its problems.

There is a good example set for us; there are many inter-racial marriages all over the world and somehow the marriages do not work and end up in divorce. In many cases single parents have to take the responsibility for bringing up their children. What about those children? The parents of those children disown them just because of their color or ask their children to leave their houses. Of course it is not normal and it is hardly even credible. It shows that people who have love for the child do not put any conditions, since there is no condition in love, it is purely devotion.

In the Western world social workers have been and are faced with the problem of discrimination between black and white children. I have met some white families with black adopted children, and they are most happy and blissful. They are taking excellent care of the children just like that they are the biological parents of the children. I met a lady and she told me the story of her adopting a black child a few years back. The main thing that she told me was the attitude of the social welfare people. They had advised her not to adopt a black child since that would bring problems in both their lives. There would be the cultural problem and as the child would grow up, there would be ample questions on the differences of the skin color and the child would demand answers. While this great lady was telling me the story she was also tending her black child who incidentally was quite ill that day. The way she was caring for the child, the worry, and the look of affection in her eyes clearly showed how much she loved the child, regardless of the color. It also showed her greatness, sensibility and humility. I felt very proud to see such an interaction between the mother and the adopted child with a different skin color. Coming back to her story, I found it very ridiculous that the bureaucratic agencies were playing such a negative role in child adoption, rather than encouraging the people and try to solve the problems of adoption. They are creating more problems and certainly society does not need, that this type of approach by people in authority is a negative influence and is unhelpful to all. Why are the authorities focusing on the forthcoming issues? Why do they not respect people's feelings? Why does it create a problem to intermingle people of different skin color? On the other hand we are speaking daily against racism. What a sweet contradiction! These questions need to be answered. The lady further told me that she was quite glad of her decision and had no problems whatsoever. I was delighted to hear this - it showed to me that there are still many sensible and humane people in the world who are broad-minded enough to look beyond the skin color of children and see them as tiny human beings wanting to be cared for.

Since I noticed that the relevant agencies discouraged people adopting children from other races, I thought it would be a nice idea to meet people who are adopting children other than their own race. Now the issue is, how do the children think themselves when they get older? I have met a few children of different ages and their thinking is all the same. They are very happy and feel they have no problems arising from their skin color. They strongly believe they should know the culture of the society they live in. The question arises here how to be aware of the culture? The only way, I think, is to live in that society and be aware of the traditions and customs prevailing there, rather than to read about it in books, magazines and newspapers and then make strong statements about the culture. It is a fact that reality is quite different from bookish knowledge. By living in the situation, one can know the truth and the logic of any statement that one makes would then be powerful. The people who judge on hearing stories only are doubtful and can never know the reality. They can only make uneducated statements of that particular place and the culture and as we all know ' little knowledge is always dangerous'.

If people from the other countries decide to go to America, it is quite likely that they might face different kinds of problems but their next generation will not face any of those cultural and language barriers, for them it will be home and we can observe that is the case. Is it necessary to put such conditions on people for adoption? I believe that we need to go for adoption on merit basis and try to bring up all the children all over the world in the same way, since we are all human beings and there should not be any other race prevailing in this world other than the human race. Later on then we may find that statistics will show an improvement on the current sad situation.

CONCEPT OF FREEDOM

I AM STAYING IN THE NETHERLANDS and probably will stay for a few more years; I call it my headquarters for the time-being. A head office, naturally has more rights as compared to its branches, no matter how large and functional they are. Now, whenever one thinks of Holland, what comes to one's mind is windmills, tulips, the traditional wooden shoes (clog's) and dairy products. I felt I knew Holland before I got here as a result of these traditions. By the way I personally like the tulips and dairy products. I have eaten different kinds of cheese all over the world but I found the Dutch 'jonge kaas' to be really yummy.

The Netherlands is also very famous for its liberal attitude; the young can get money in a very early age like other Western countries and can live an independent life. Everybody has his own rights, in this country homosexuals have full rights as well. Both the media and the law-making authorities are giving them their full attention and helping them. I am not sure whether they are helping them but certainly they are giving them full coverage which they have never got in former times. It was all taboo even a decade back but now it appear to be highly fashionable.

By using the word 'fashionable' I do do not intend to insult anyone but it is quite evident that nowadays there are so many people coming out from the so-called closet. I am afraid I have used the terminology 'closet', I am still wondering how big that closet was and is? Coming out from the closet they are getting the top most attention, sometimes locally and in some cases throughout the country. It looks people who were hidden for a long long time, all of a sudden have rather too many rights. They are trying to compensate since there was not much freedom for them to publicly declare their views in the past and now they can say whatever they want. Actually these people existed but they had suppressed their feelings somehow I am told.

Nowadays due to liberty of thought more and more people are coming out. I am not going into detail since a lot of people are already engaged in this topic whether it is natural or it is normal behavior. But I would certainly say most human beings are attracted towards the same sex at a certain age or time but that does not mean that they have to experiment and cross all the boundaries to gain personal experience. That could be a conscious and sub-conscious fight within oneself. It could be the reason, at certain stage one likes the same gender only because one wishes to be like that person. It could be purely a psychological reason than otherwise. To have an attraction with the same sex and have a friendship is quite different than to have a crush. That is what people have learned from the ancient civilization and naturally through their respective religions as well. Does our move away from the traditional religious adherences cause destruction in our lifestyle? Should those in authoritative positions in the hierarchies reflect in their own attitudes and behavior patterns? These may be valid questions.

In other countries, these people do have rights but they have not been fully accepted socially and the media does not give them priority as they are getting in a few Western countries only. This shows that the straight people (the ones still in the closet) are still hesitant to accept them and their governments are giving importance to the majority and have not changed their policies simply for the satisfaction of a few people in the society. The Dutch bureaucracy is more courteous and their point of view is that they have to care for each and every sort of person in the society. They are trying to provide every facility to everyone so that their citizens can be satisfied, relaxed and happy. It is like they are providing a facility to the people who are on drugs. People on drugs can get certain kinds of drugs from the prescribed places legally. There are coffee shops which can sell drugs, but otherwise in Holland there is a ban on drugs. They do not want to promote drugs, they are doing their best to control the situation and that is the way they have adopted.

The idea is, to take care of other Dutch citizens who do not want to be disturbed by the drug-users. Is it working ? We have to be honest about that. They do not want the people have problems and be victims of frustration. So what is happening, the government is really trying to mother the whole society and doing its best to keep every child happy. In this world it is very rare to keep every person fully satisfied with life. We all know that there is no limit on satisfaction, therefore it looks that we are challenging the law of nature. Now what would be the outcome, we have to wait and see. I would not be surprised that very soon people would start thinking about God. Though nowadays it is fashionable almost all over the world that people are denying the Creator and have their own self-fabricated ideas about life. Will denial give them their peace? Are they peaceful? We need to think about that, don't we? One thing is sure if they are peaceful then there must be lot of love every where in the world. And that is hard to find.

Coming back to my point of view, which certainly does need more explanation, I would say that the authority's role here is just like those parents who fulfill every demand of their children. But then the children grow up to be spoilt and misbehave in society. When they want something and they can not have access to it, they then try to get it through criminal ways, because that has been their upbringing. They had been getting everything they had asked their parents and are not used to being refused and compromising. They think that it is their right to obtain all the things they desire. Now who is to be blamed then, the parents or the children? The parents forgot to teach their children the very lesson of being satisfied with what you have and to work hard to fulfill your wishes. In the same way I get the idea that the government is leading the people to believe that anything they wish for can be fulfilled immediately by them. Is that possible? Can we meet all human wishes?

On the other hand, there are those parents who fulfill the basic needs of their children and on the children's demand for further things, they explain that perhaps they can not afford it or that it is not good for the children to have those things at that particular stage. In this way they promote positive thinking and the other approach to life. The children then fully believe in practical things and lead sensible way of life. They gradually start learning how to react when the responses are not favorable. They know definitely that everything is not possible and they have to learn how to cope with the situation when things do not go the way they want it. In this case, both the children and the parents have communication and are trying to be happy by making each other happy.. In the first case the parents are always in trouble and never come out with good conclusion. It is just like one-way traffic, and it is hard to get positive results.

I would now say that bureaucracy has to think about the good of all the society and not the specific few groups, and should not force people to know all the things happening around them. Sometimes it is far better not to know a few things than to know everything, since evil always has more attraction than the good things. My Dutch buddies, with whom I had a detailed discussion on this topic, had the collective point of view that there was nothing wrong in promoting homosexual activities. Their strong point was that they were also human beings and should be taken care of as any other human being. It is just like a child born into any religion has the right to be of that religion. So children have no fault at all in belonging to their various beliefs. Most of us would certainly be convinced with this way of thinking since there is no difference between all human beings. I strongly believe everyone has the right to live and it is every human's duty to take care of others. We should not hurt anyone simply because of color, gender or belief. But at the same time we have to be sure that we are not provoking others and we are not violating others' spiritual peace.

I agree with the logic of taking care of the homosexual children, but does it mean that we have to promote them through media. O.K we need to cover to some extent to let the world know what is happening around. Then it is just like information which everybody has the right to know. But in my opinion, if the media gives powerful coverage then there will be no way to control this flaw in society. To provide information can be a service and favor for society, but to overdo it, could be a big confusion for the rest of the world. We need to think about that. Also, it would show that both the media and the respective authorities are not working in favor of society so they have no business trying to keep control on any part of society. We know that to be over conscientious about society does not work in its favor. So the bureaucracy has to be very careful and active to first control negativity and then minimize it as much as possible.

Here, I have to mention that doctors have conceded to the fact that homosexuality is one of the major causes of the most dreaded disease AIDS - Acquired Immune Deficiency Syndrome, so we really have to be extra careful. The Dutch bureaucracy particularly should not think partially, but should have a collective approach so that they can work positively on the solution and save the Dutch society from imminent disaster. This is definitely beneficial for the people and country. At the present stage, only the bureaucracy can properly control this factor and afterwards other social services can work on this project and be helpful.

HOW YOUNG BLACKS FEEL

THESE ARE THE FEELINGS OF a young black man in political asylum in one of the First world countries. I met him in the camp where he was living with other people from different countries. It was a nice environment particularly for those people who like to know more about other cultures. But to be a part of the camp is certainly a different experience. I met him in his room and he looked so desperate lying down on his bed that I invited him to come downstairs and together we would have some coffee. It was really none of my business to probe into his affairs but I never can resist helping anyone in a desperate situation. On asking him the reason for his unhappiness, he extemporaneously replied why I was so keen to know. His quick response made sense to me at the same time made me feel more close to him, and I asked him to go out with me for a drink and he agreed.

We went to the nearest bar and I ordered coffee for both of us. While drinking we were talking about different issues since I wanted to make him more relaxed so that I could talk with him on the real problem. During the discussion I saw the way his eyes lit up and life came into them, he started looking more relaxed and casual. That gave me the feeling that he was feeling more normal, as I know a few black people who are always very casual in their behavior when they are feeling nice and calm. That is I believe, one of their important characteristics. They can not hide themselves for a long time and that is the very opposite to the Western world. Well! I started questioning him about his feelings living in the white surroundings where about everyone had no time for each other as he reckoned. Since he was black in color, he then automatically had a slim chance of being granted the status he wanted. That was his opinion too as I had guessed from our discussion.

He opened up to me and told me of his loneliness and that he had only black friends. What he wanted most to get a decent job as soon as possible and then to get married to a white girl. On one hand I was glad to know his goal but the same time I asked him, why a white girl, why not a black lady? Furthermore I told him that I like a person with whom I can sing together in all areas of life and I do not care for the color. He thought I meant again a girl from my own country, but I corrected his statement and clarified to him, any girl from anywhere. I tried my level best to convince him that there was no difference between him and me, but his impulsive reply was to say that if he had a skin color like mine, which is brown, he would have no problem in socializing with ladies of white color. Well, that was the way he thought. I am not exposing this conversation to praise brown skin or to denounce any other, but to show how the young black people think and feel on the whole about this particular issue.

The young want to communicate and interact with each other and do not want to involve any racism in their relationships. The black youth still feel that the white people have some hostility towards them, though it is quite evident that things are getting much better than before. Our older generations were different than today's young generation, but the bureaucracy is still holding stiff policies. But overall we get the impression that people do not really bother with these kinds of issues. Perhaps nowadays with all the technology stuff they have found other ways to make themselves busy. Is it true that people who were opposing other people in the former times had more time? That is why they had to find some issue to burn their energies, and sometimes when they do not find any real problem they then fabricate one to keep themselves busy. I believe they were very smart people, they had taken good care of their time and did not spoil even one bit of it. Is this the case?

I am taking the privilege here, to talk of the political asylum-seekers in different countries of the industrial world. Most of them, unfortunately were black people whose countries were in trouble those days. We are very aware of the condition of Africa and Iraq as well. I had met some people living in the asylum camps and they told me about the shortage of space for them. The concerned governments had made arrangements for them in old tourist hotels, caravans and the old people houses. Now, what I noticed was that it was the general impression that the authorities favored people from certain parts of the world. Well, was that true? I do not know. But surely some of the people felt they were being treated as second or third class. I am afraid to say the black people were on the top of the list of those who felt left out.

Their contention was that the East Europeans were getting better services and better accommodation than them. Furthermore, the foreign police tackled them rather abruptly and they did not find any peace there. They came here to get some peace in their lives which they could not get in their own countries unfortunately. All the time when they had any inquiry no one wanted to take any responsibility and referred the problem to others. They really did not know who was really responsible for their future there; the foreign police or social organizations. While I was listening to the story my heart was captivated and I was trying to get a feel the situation. Therefore I decided to learn more about the facts and figures. It was hard for me to interrogate the police and social organizations since most of the time I doubt whether they know themselves what they are talking about. I would say they have their own limits as well. It seems a very ambiguous statement, but it is the benefit of doubt I have always given to these authorities, and that is how I keep myself to remain productive as well.

I have always been keen to see the true facts myself and it was a sort of challenge for me to find out the reality in this case. The hotel I went to was owned by two brothers, the younger of which was very civilized and treated the refugees humanely. But the elder brother was the opposite and a victim of the superiority complex. He had traveled to some countries, owned a few properties and had two B.M.Ws. His style was to favor those who were impressed by him and always agreed with him. It was a pleasant incident for me to watch two different personalities with the same blood and cultural background.

I thought sometimes perhaps they had some sort of accord between themselves; how to handle the existing situation. But by talking with the elder brother I got to the impression that he had had too much success in his early life and did not know how to maintain a balanced personality. Since he was facing a terrible time of his life and did not want to expose his difficulties to others, he behaved rather aggressively towards other people. Most of the time people felt humiliated by his attitude. I would like to mention his age, he was in his late twenties. I had a detailed discussion with him in which I made known to him my few experiences and association with the people of different countries. We talked about the world since luckily I had traveled to some of the same parts which he had traveled as well. We had a really pleasant conversation, but still I do not hesitate say that he behaved snobbishly.

My idea was to communicate my point of view to him, so I went through all the preliminary process. I wanted to make him realize how people might think in different situations, so that he could easily choose his part and then I could get my answer. I gave him an example of a fruit-laden tree which was always bent and a fruitless tree which was always straight in direction. In a very friendly atmosphere, I tried to convince him to be more flexible and not to be straight all the time like fruitless tree. I tried to say he did not have to impose all his decisions on others since he knew more than other people. I made it clear to him that there is nobody in this world who can claim to know more than other human beings. It is just an accident that sometimes people know more than the others in the particular situation but that does not mean it is forever. He should discuss the facts and try to convince people through relevant arguments.

Well! I had better come back to the topic since my intentions are not to talk about his personality, but the problems the people who had taken refuge were facing. They had come due to problems in their own countries and over here were still not being given their due treatment by the social organizations. I think the United Nations really has to make the refugee problem a top priority. Though they are working very hard in every part of the world to help the needy it seems there are still some areas left to be covered. Of course the United Nations can not do anything without the help of the member countries, therefore it is the duty of the respective countries to make sure that they are dealing with the refugees on the standard merit. The astonishing and the strange thing which came to my notice was that the refugees from Iraq were treated differently from the others, simply because the one and only great super power was against their country. I do not understand that specific policy. Should we have to discriminate among refugees as well?

Once anyone decides to seek refuge in any other place that means one has a problem about one's own identity and survival. Then what is the fun to discriminate, all hands are already up. The question was raised in the beginning as to whether people from East Europe are treated differently and far better than the other refugees. I can not give any authentic statement about that, but I know that most of the East European refugees are involved in lawless activities like stealing etc. They are in Western Europe simply to make more money and they concentrate solely on their major goal and are not a bit worried about survival

Classification of real refugees is needed by the United Nations so that the people in genuine need of help can be handled properly. Also the discrimination among refugees should be stopped by the organizations and everyone should be handled on merit basis. Perhaps in this way we can keep the refugee problem in control so that it will not be a big problem for the country itself. In fact this is happening, only because of defective policies in the system. I would like to mention, most of the refugees are simple and innocent people looking for better survival. They get side tracked only due to unnecessary obstacles and obvious discrimination.

TRUST IN RELATIONSHIPS

I WAS LIVING IN THE VRIJ university hostel in Amsterdam at one stage and there I met a very sensible girl, who showed me a very bitter side of trust and relationship in the Western culture - it was her own sad experience in her early twenties. Why I am saying the Western culture because she was Dutch, and I would say it is quite usual to find this kinds of evidence in the Western world than in the Eastern countries. I had often seen her sitting alone at her table and I could feel that there was something amiss.

One day I was also sitting alone at my table, therefore I asked her if I could sit with her. She agreed nicely and we initiated a discussion on various issues. She certainly was competent in the field of discussion and showed herself to be quite good-natured and thoughtful. I had never seen her cursing people or gossiping and chatting in company about other students, which is quite something, particularly in the students' hostels. Life in the hostels is very colorful and the gossips are as good as Hollywood. In that sort of environment she always kept herself aloof and seemed to enjoy solitude. We went on talking about all the world and around midnight I asked her permission to finish and leave. Her reply, telling me to go while she would stay on, seemed to be quite rude, but I realized it was not so, for I had sensed in her a great depression and she seemed to me on the verge of tears.

I sat down again. She asked me why I was wasting my time with her and I told her that she reminded me of my sister and talking to her seemed to me like I was with my own sister. On hearing this the tears threatening to overflow, came out and she started crying. This was all very embarrassing for me and I did not know how to comfort her. After a bout of tears, she told me about her own family. She had two brothers, but had never seen any love from them. So I thought at that particular moment, she was in some difficulty and that it could be a financial one. Financial problems are actually part and parcel of any student life and particularly when one is caught into that bad patch, believe me, everything looks rotten and one starts hating everything and everyone without any solid reasons. It is very common among students and perhaps from the way I asked her she might have remembered her own family but the facts were quite different.

She told me she was the only daughter in the family and her two brothers had never accepted her. When she was only fourteen her father and both the brothers abused her. They had never respected her mother as well, one day she woke up and her mother was not there. She ran away from home and left her alone with them. She did not leave any note for her either and she had no clue where she was now. After her mum left her family had not liked her and they did not behave well with her. She had felt abused all the time therefore she had run away from home as well. Now whenever the scene came to mind she could not control herself and was searching ways to keep going, which was very hard sometimes. She was not in a position to do anything against them because she did not want to ruin the rest of her life. She had never done anything against them but she was afraid that they would come here any time and would hurt her again.

I sat stunned and quiet as she went on with her tragic story. Her family had shattered her and abused her in every sense, and she never knew the reason for their behavior. It is hard to understand how she was coping with this life where her own blood has cheated her. She was now all alone in this world, abandoned by her own family. Now, at twenty she lived with a deep mistrust and hatred for all men, which is very annoying but very understandable in her situation. No one was really there for her, now she needed help but she did not have anyone to trust, even her own mother had no connection with her. But she was not against her mother and did not say why. I told her that her mother too was guilty of neglecting her and not caring for her or talking with her. Her ambiguous reply was that her mother had not done anything wrong to her in her life.

This was quite a lengthy debate. But I did not want to disturb her anymore for I felt she had already enough miseries. Sometimes I think that the reason she was not against her mother was that she understood her mothers pain since they were both women. Perhaps that was the love of the daughter towards her mother since she had seen her in pain as well. Sometimes it is very confusing, but is it not the case that the mother was grown-up in this relationship so she should think more for her daughter's security than herself? She was the one who was equally responsible for bringing her into this world. Then again when one's own life is in jeopardy it can be hard for one to think of others. But I always believed and still am a strong believer in motherly love. There is no such love like mother's love in the entire world, it is devoted and unconditional. Perhaps she believes in the same values as well, that is why she did not want to think against her. But what kind of mother was she? Why do these kind of incidents happen more and more nowadays?

And again what kind of father was he? Was he a monster? I am using this word deliberately since I have never found such values in the human history but certainly these indications can be found in special kind of monsters. The worrying aspect is the two youngsters who were involved in this violence as well. I am not blaming them that harshly because naturally the role model for them was the father, and they had seen so much violence at home and now they perhaps had come to the stage that it seemed normal to them. Like a lot of other things which are becoming more normal than before. It appears that the 'closet' was really very big and strong. It could be the reason that the father had a very difficult childhood and had some sort of hostility towards women and he went so far for his revenge that he even forgot the basics of civilization. For me it was a really horrifying moment and

I could not say anything to her. But certainly I can blame society and its liberalism.

After this discussion and listening to her tragic story, I do not agree with the so-called Western liberty. If such liberty involves destroying your own kith and kin's lives, then I would go for the more solid Eastern culture, including that of the Eastern Europeans where people have still some values. The tabloid goes on promoting the Western culture with its liberalism and showing that it is more adoptable in this modern world; but what of its increasing negative values? These certainly arise from too much liberty. As far as I know liberty should be to the extent that everyone is fully secure in life and has no fear of expression. Danger, not only in physical violence but in destroying the very lives of the people in every sense. Excess of everything is bad and leads to evil. It is my firm belief that we need to put a limit on liberty; there should be a certain limit and some criteria so one can not exceed one's limits. The Western people certainly view the word limitation with bad grace, but there are too many problems arising now. Before the situation gets totally out of hand, we should go through the arduous task of controlling the flaws, irrespective of which culture we belong to. Human relationships and families are far too sacred to be destroyed by the threat of the evil influence of excess liberty.

LONG HAIR SMALL BRAINS

THE WESTERNERS ARE TRYING TO impose their own culture in every single part of the world. They are making every effort to prove their culture is better than the Eastern culture or any other; and they are thus researching different ways of proving their superiority. That makes sense to me, it is logical; when one has money one wants more money, when one has power one wants more power. Because the Western world has both money and power therefore they want everything. There is as such no certain limit and the sky is the limit for them perhaps. That is why nowadays things are moving and traveling faster than ever in the history of mankind. I would say psychologically, if they are really thought to be on the upper side by the others then they do not have to prove or show their superiority.

Entering the Western world I have noticed quite a strange point of view - that people who have long hair usually possess small brains! I hope Westerners will deny this concept since the tabloid is promoting this general opinion. When I first heard of this opinion I certainly was quite curious to know all about this matter. I had seen a feature on television about the Eastern women with the topic 'long hair small brains'. These days mostly it is the Eastern women who are viewed as having long hair. After listening carefully I noticed that the discussion was actually all about the Eastern women and their attitude towards the practical world. I would say that in this case we should bring some men in the picture as well since it is very normal in the Western culture for men to grow their hair long. But this concept in the Western world is only about women and for men it is perhaps just a fashion so I would try and confine myself to that only.

Rather than to discuss the pros and cons of this topic, I would mention the views of the Western women themselves who go for long hair. I had given myself an assignment to collect the general views of the people and asked a few people about this topic but the responses were very different from those presented by T.V. The lady to whom I posed this question, answered me rather abruptly that, rather than to discuss such a silly topic, she could arrange some other work for me to do! She refused to talk further about it and went away. She thought perhaps I was doing some research work and was using my energies for nothing and I had better get another job. Well, since that was not the case but even then I wanted to know more views of the people. But at the same time, like most of the people say, the first impression is the last impression, now I was a little bit concerned about the people's reactions as well. I have no desire to be insulted or insulting but my curiosity did not allow me to leave the topic alone.

Certainly I was very careful about discussing this topic with any other lady. I do believe that everyone has their self-respect! But I did not stop this mission and after a careful survey of women with both long and short hair, the result showed that no one really believed in this concept and most of them thought it was rather stupid and disgusting to have such a point of view. I wanted next to ask the opinion of the Eastern women, but I thought that perhaps a revolutionary Eastern woman would probably kill me, since Eastern women with long hair are in the majority. Of course I am joking, indeed I do have the courage to go through such an interview with them! Which I did. But most of them just laughed at me and smiled. I got message by body language only, so did others I believe.

The people who are actively involved in these activities and are trying to segregate the people and create a big gulf among the two cultures, should certainly be stopped. This is a totally negative value for any culture to possess. I am sure my readers would agree with me and would discourage this issue. It is not possible to give any statement about a person's intelligence simply by looking at the length of the hair or any part of the body. It is quite ridiculous and rather humiliating. I really appreciate the patience of the Eastern women and some Western women who have long hair. I do appreciate the men as well who have long hair though they are and were not part of the discussion. The length of one's hair is totally a personal matter and if to have long beautiful hair adds to the beauty of a person, then why is there any criticism about it? We better learn how to be realistic rather than to believe in different kinds of superstition.

The bureaucracy does think about issues and groups of people, particularly the homosexuals, then why not the people who are being criticized or looked down just because they happen to have long hair. This is the opinion of a woman with long hair. Why does the bureaucracy allow the humiliation of such people and have nothing to say about it? They should set this issue right and should denounce such pathetic thinking.

FIGHTING FOR SATISFACTION

I N LIFE EVERYONE RIGHTLY WANTS to achieve their targets and obtain their satisfaction. But there are many cases when people have accomplished their goals yet they are still not content or happy. This can be due to the impulsiveness of human nature. The satisfaction then varies at different stages; one can say impulsiveness is inherent in mankind and it is like a pressure on people to work for the desired result in their lives.

While I was a graduate student, my friends and I had the opinion that there were too many restrictions in the Eastern culture and we wanted to know why we were so different from others because we could not date and could not go to the bars and discos. By the way, there is no bar and disco concept in some places. There are still places where people might not even be familiar with these words. In Eastern countries, where they do have these facilities it is not permissible to do anything freely. I mean friendships with the opposite gender is taboo, to go in mixed parties is not encouraged in most of the countries. The funny thing is most of them really want it, but it is just the double standards of the society which stops them from going further. Whenever certain groups of people want to create any environment or a step further to match the Western world, these moves are rejected very strongly by the so-called fundamentalists.

It is not wrong to believe in any fundamentals and to be a fundamentalist. But it is totally wrong when one is a terrorist or involved in inhuman activities and gets the shelter of any religion. These people are not fundamentalists, they are terrorists. All the prevailing cultures and religions in the Eastern part teach us how to love and care for other human beings. If they have learned everything from their respective beliefs and religions then how come the fundamentalists are involved in the killing and are certainly cannibals. Societies should take strong action against them.

Also the cinema and the theatre are not places for girls. We had attended and arranged many forums where we discussed the liberty of boys and girls. Many of my friends gave examples of the Western culture and everyone agreed that if we had more liberty in our culture then perhaps that would ease young people's frustration. At that time I used to give lectures on culturalism though I do confess that I had no experience of other cultures. And now, at this stage when I have traveled and seen other cultures and I am living within the Western culture, my knowledge is different now. I have seen that the young people over here are have the same problems. I am not talking about only 'liberal' children. By liberal I mean those teenagers who have left their parents and are living on their own. How they manage is another story. I would say that because the parents have a totally liberal attitude their children have gone astray. In fact such children then have parents only in name. I would call this situation an exceptional one though it is getting more and more common. But still people do not encourage this behavior and it is not yet accepted by the society as well. If parents do not give them the required attention and care, the children then retaliate and start rebellious activities. Here, I would say that it is totally the parents' fault.

All religions emphasize the importance of the parents giving top priority to their children and fulfilling their duty. In this modern era, couples are living together and are not entering into marriage. It is becoming normal in the Western society nowadays that people would prefer to live with each other before entering into wedlock. Every country has different rules and regulations for this difacto relationship.

It is getting more and more popular as they think it is decreasing the rate of divorces. I have my great doubts about that, as the statistics show as well. Well, we should first think about our own life but when we have children then we should think about them in the same way. Mostly the couples living together think that they have taken the right of decision not to marry and are happy with their life style, and they often do have children during their relationships before even being officially married. In such relationships both of them had had a chance to live together before actually getting married legally. They share everything and live like married couples, they expect from their spouses the same care as in the case in the marriages but they are not officially bound. Not all the relationships go on well and break-ups occur. They then find they have each other, but are not 'in love' with each other and thus are not living comfortably. They start looking and finding other ways for peace which they might or might not get, but the children are always victims in all situations.

In most of the cases children go with the mothers. Some mothers, when their babies grow up, think that their own lives are more important than to look after the children and they usually find some new love in their lives. According to them their own rights are too important to give priority to their own children . But then what about the left-behind children? Now they have no real parents around them. Of course they are getting the basic necessities of life - food, cloths and education. But what about real love, care and attention? These are very vital elements in any human life particularly for the child. These are our major characteristics and that is why we are better than other living creatures on this planet.

A child is just like a flower and should be treated with tender love and care and to be touched gently. Just as flowers bring joy to us so do children and nothing compares to the joy they bring to us. If the flower itself is partly or fully dead then how can people enjoy it. The same is the case with the nourishment of children; if they do not get the basic elements of being loved then what is society expecting from them. Certainly when they grow up they will get revenge from their elders, which they should since it is the law of nature. Then parents and the older generation have no right to blame or criticize them, as the saying goes ' as you sow so shall you reap'.

O.K for a moment if we consider that, not marrying and living together may have solved the problem of divorce but then the children's lives need also to be saved and given proper thought. No religion or culture allows us to play with human lives and in fact when parents do not take responsibility of their children they are then playing with their lives and humanity on the whole. Parents do have to control their own wishes and desires and give priority to their children since they are responsible for bringing them in this world; it sounds a very fair deal to me. Everyone wants to exceed their limits and get their own personal satisfaction, and that is always at the expense of others who are then put into trouble. We should take time off to think and care for others and find ways to help them get their own satisfaction. Then we would build up a good and caring world around us and thus put a stop to the ugly faces of selfishness, classification and frustration.

HUMAN INTELLIGENCE

WE ALWAYS HEAR ABOUT THE intelligence and genius of people which are essential aspects of the human being. We also hear about philanthropists involved in altruistic activities. They always look at things in a positive way and are always thinking for the benefit of humanity. People look up to the great personalities and quite often choose their names for their children; in the hope that their children would grow up and justify the personalities attached to those names. This shows the strong desire of the parents for the progress of their children.

Everyone also prays to God for their prosperity and progress. Here an important point must be taken into account - people tend to forget God when they have achieved what they always prayed for, they then start pretending that it was purely their own efforts and God had nothing to do with it. We are aware of the fact that God always knows the inner feelings and thoughts of every single person; especially when the outer actions of people person are in total juxtaposition to the innermost emotions. But even then people are complaining that God never listens to their prayers and desires and when they are not satisfied they then start questioning God. I would say perhaps such people are not familiar with the saying - 'God helps those who help themselves'.

First one has to make every efforts for oneself, just like if one wants a good job one should keep researching on one's own and always plan as best as one can. Then surely if one is all-meaningful and earnest with oneself, God will come to one's aid in fulfilling the targets. How can God come to anyone's help if no one can even move for their own self. We can change our fate with our good planning and struggles, but certainly without struggle there is no chance to get any divine help and it is rather useless to blame God or anyone else.

In most cases, people are not working themselves, and are very optimistic in saying that," God will help us". How it is possible? How can God come and move them to bring some food for themselves? What God really does, is to put some ways and suggestions into one's mind so that one can easily get one's target and we can call this intuition. Furthermore I would say, when one borrows something or money from loved ones, one would always plan how to ask and then how to return that favor as well. For that, mostly people spend their days and nights to present their case so that they cannot be refused, even if they have to use very artificial language and praise for the person from whom they need to get some aid. Sometimes they are successful and sometimes they are not. In both the scenarios they will encourage or discourage themselves rather than the person from whom they were planning to get some help. What does that mean? Does it show that people do know how to react in the situation when the things do not go their way or it is just a coincidence. Now when we are asking money from another human being we are so polite and rational or rather pretending to be rational. Why cannot we be rational in the case of God?

God is people's inner peace; people who have peace in their life can be sure that God is with them, otherwise it is virtually impossible. It is very easy to criticize God because, in the first place, it is fashionable nowadays and secondly, people think that nothing will harm them by violating the religious laws or condemning God. But that is not true, we are facing so many troubles nowadays which mankind had never come across before. We have to look back into history to see that there were so many philosophers and scientists who had done their best to disprove the existence of God but none of them yet have proven he does not exist.

To minimize denial they would say that there is a super power that exists but whether it is God or anything else they are not sure. I believe they are equally responsible in misleading humanity and that is why people are so confused, they are not sure what to believe and what to trust. On top of all this the religious people have given so many bad examples for mankind, that people feel alien to them and this is the only major reason that these ideas took hold. It is all very confusing and painful. It is hard for the one who is in the situation but at the same time we know for sure that nobody can sail in two boats, we have to decide ourselves and have to make our choices. It is very normal that when there is a hole in a glass it is hard to keep water in it; the same is the case with the religious people who have created so much confusion and hatred among human beings that people are reluctant to even believe in any God. Most of them are feeling betrayed and cheated. Now whose job is it and what do we have to think?

In the former times when people were believing in various religions and God they were not very impulsive, though impulsiveness is a part of human nature, but they were getting their peace through practicing their religions. If the situation did not go in their favor they still thought that God had saved them from some big disaster. It was just a matter of strong belief. It might sound very conservative to the new generation. Let us say if one is in love with anyone, one will feel that everything is so perfect and complete and in some cases one might think life is heaven for oneself, and certainly it does not matter what other people think or say. It is certain that other people can not visualize the way lovers are seeing the world at that particular moment.

Everything has its own fun and people have different criticism about that, some will say that one is stupid and some will say let one to enjoy it since life is very short. But then why do people just pray and get impulsive and when the decision is not in their favor they start complaining and giving excuses like God was not happy with them. What I do not understand is why can not they think in positive terms

- perhaps the refusal was better in those circumstances or perhaps they had not worked hard enough or prayed the right way and next time they would do better. Would you fight with your love only because they have not helped you, and if you adopt those ways of life then it would be not far when there will be nobody for you. Then do you think you have the right to blame! Yes, certainly you, yourself.

The majority of this world believes in God and everyone has their own way of expression - their praying and worshipping style can be different but it is as certain as death that God loves every single human being irrespective of the color, race and the social status. If this statement is not true and there is any doubt in anyone's mind then I can tell you all the rich people of the world would never let themselves die and vanish from this materialistic and colorful world. There is no point in challenging God. People choose to hide the dark side of their nature and this side has prevented them reaching their goal.

WHAT A DIFFERENCE

I AM ALWAYS IN SEARCH OF different things which can be helpful for my friends and in this case, for my readers as well. I did find something of this kind in the lush Dutch countryside. I was in Zaanstad, though the residents of that area would not call it countryside since it is very close to Amsterdam. By any standard Amsterdam is not a countryside since one can find rather more of anything than one really wants or desires. But I would say Zaanstad is still categorically the countryside. Anyway I loved it and I lived there for a while, and almost daily I went for a walk. It was very calm and peaceful to walk there especially in the evenings. One day I saw a very conspicuous poster hanging on a normal-looking house. I simply had to read it, just like a child has to drink milk, whether he likes it or not. That poster played the same role as milk for me - it was food for thought.

I am creating suspense about what was written on the poster since it was a cultural shock for me and thus took me sometime to describe it. The unique poster was about the silver jubilee of a couple for whom it was now the twenty-fifth year of their marriage or difacto relationship without any sort of separation, I believe. This was big news in the Western culture and definitely it is, that was one of the reasons they were celebrating the precious moment. Since I am writing this book for people who belong to the Eastern culture as well and I know many people do not know the meaning of living together yet; then here I will just give the layout. This is the condition of those people who do not want to enter into marriage straight away but feel that they can live with each other. This mode of behavior is becoming very popular nowadays in the Western world. For them it is better to live together than to marry, actually in the back of their mind people do not want to lose their relationship. It has been noticed that people get along very nicely with each other while they are just friends and the moment they decide to get involved or to get married then all of a sudden the relationships turns into a disaster, of which the probability is getting more and more. It could be the people's fear which is stopping them from getting married nowadays than in the former times.

I did ask a few of my good friends who were living together with their partners. According to them, they did not want to bind themselves with any person without getting to know them thoroughly first. And there is no telling how long it takes to 'know' each other. I do know many couples who have been living together for three years and more and still think that they need more time. It is a fact that we are born selfish, but it is hard to say whether that is a selfish decision or a practical one. Certainly when it works it is a practical decision and the moment it does not work then maybe it is a selfish decision, it is as simple as that. At the same time we know it is hard to accept that we are selfish though it is easy to point out. Another thing which has always been a confusing question to me, that why do we love our pets more than human beings? I am still maintaining this point of view. I have no intention of discouraging people who love their pets are dear to them, but still in a fair amount of the world humanity is suffering. Do we not have to do our duties first then have our pleasure?

Thus with such realities around me particularly in the Western world, if I may say, I feel really proud of those kinds of posters which convey some important messages and which, I think is good canvassing as well, so that at least the people living in that area could think on that life style as well. I feel very moved to write about the couple who stayed together for twenty-five years not only to hang that poster outside their home, but also to show the community and the youngsters that it is still possible to maintain a healthy relationship. I would not be surprised to hear that they had good and bad moments in their relationship as that is an indication of a good and colorful life. There should be some ups and downs in life so that people can keep working to make it better. For sure there will be no fun if every move of life is predictable. Actually what is happening is we are becoming very easy going, lazy and more materialistic nowadays, that is why we do not have the patience to hang on during the hardships of life.

Everyone wants a wonderful life but no one is really ready to put some energy into it, like my respectable couple did. In all circumstances I would give credit to them. The aspect here which does compel me to think or write about is the differences of thought and opinion of human kind in different parts of the world. Sometimes it is hard to believe that we are living in one world and on the same planet. In one part of the world people are living together for so many years just to 'know' each other before entering into a legal relationship, whereas in another part of the world most people marry without fully knowing each other and then it takes them the same time period to get out of their situation.

The perturbing factor here is the contrast - of two extreme situations - and who is right and who is wrong is the cardinal question. Now how can we overcome these problems? The probable solution will vary according to the environmental situation, as we can not determine the same rules and regulations for both the respective cultures. However the common point of discussion is that both of them are working for a better life and are trying their best to come out with appropriate solutions for the situation. But at the same time everyone is thinking on individual basis and not collectively and that is why more problems are cropping up. It is a fact that we do not really have any mutual and collective thinking. We do know we have too much love inside and we need only the right direction.

When we talk about the Third world countries, since most of the Eastern part of the world is still considered to be developing, it is quite evident that people are have a lack of resources and that can be monetary, education and awareness itself. But here in the Western world things should be different, though sometimes some events make me ask whether it is right or not. I would mention the opinion of a Dutch acquaintance with whom I was discussing the poster. His reply surprised me and the words he uttered were, " Really is it so, and where?" But what was important was his expressions which was his real comment on the story about the poster. Sometimes the expression of the people and their extempore replies give them away, especially those people with a 'white' skin. Their faces are more expressive than those of the colored people. At least they can hide their real feelings through the advantage of their color. Let us be positive and consider this as a big advantage. It makes me say that what a difference of life there is in this so-called big world.

RAPID CHANGES

THE TWENTIETH CENTURY HAS SEEN many rapid changes and hence its importance. In this modern era, we have seen women rulers in the Islamic countries, the failure and the disasters of communism, war among the people of the same religion, conversion of mosques to temples, conversion of churches to discos and a lot more.

But these are some of the most vital changes occurring around us in these modern times. The most conspicuous have been the Iran-Iraq war and the Gulf war. The war between Iran and Iraq, two Islamic countries, was to prove their superiority to each other. The Gulf war started with Iraq invading a fellow Muslim country, Kuwait and ended with full interference of the 'world police' the U.S.A. The astonishing factor is that according to the Muslim religion, two Muslims groups are not supposed to fight and in any circumstances there is no allowance for killing each other. If that is right then it is a shame to say that in both these situations the great Muslim countries were involved and at the same time they are preaching to the world about Islamisation. What message are they then trying to give to the world? Their coming generations are totally confused and influenced by the Western methodology. The actions of their elders are contradictory to their sayings, therefore their base is getting weaker and weaker day by day. Why are they blaming other cultures and why are they afraid of their forthcoming generations? They should not be afraid of anything as they are aware of what they are doing and they are by no means innocent either. That is why a major part of the world is confused about their actions and reactions. It does not make any sense to me as well, maybe it does to them.

The destruction of the Barbary mosque in Delhi by the Hindus showed the never-ending hatred between the extremists Hindus and Muslim in India. In the Western world, the conversion of churches to discos is the example of the fast changing trends. I do know a few places where such incidents have occurred. One such church is situated in Zaandam, one of the oldest places in Holland. Since it has been noticed that people actually get tired of old things and the same life style, they normally then start looking for changes and start getting new things and varieties. Maybe, this is also the reason in the case of the church. Perhaps the people were fed up of that old place and wanted some dynamic change, but I have reasonable doubts.

Well, what really is bothering me is, how can people accept that a place where they and their forefathers had prayed through the ages is now converted to a pub and disco, which is a so-called sin in most religions. The religions do not allow drinking therefore I believe the conversion of church into disco is a very pleasant contrast. By the way in that specific place I have seen that people were using drugs quite freely as well. I sometimes think are we in the changing process or are we totally changed? What I still do not understand is under which circumstances can churches be converted over to discos. It could be that people wanted to get rid of many churches or the condition of the churches are deteriorating in such way that they have to dispose of the place.

O.k. if the second option is true then why are we still making new churches in the same areas and why do we not protect our own holy places, as I have learned that the places where people practice their religions are holy places and lots and lots of them get so much peace and think that they are being blessed. Now what I am trying to understand is what are those factors which make people willing to hand over their holy places to anyone solely for business reasons or otherwise, and what about the emotional and religious affiliations. Are they not powerful enough to stop us from making decisions based totally on material purposes or are we so calculated in all aspects that we are even evaluating our prayers as well. This could be one of the reasons why we are so far from spiritual peace. It is hard to understand that in one part of the world there is lot of bloodshed going on over the holy places and in the other part people are having such relaxed attitudes. And to me both ways sound very extremist.

I have come across the residents of Zaandam quite a few times and have had the opportunity to study their attitude. I would here say that they do need changes and whether they want or not is another question. They certainly are quite interesting people and sometimes I got the impression that they are complex to a certain extent, since they have not figured out their identities yet. As they are very near to Amsterdam, they think that they are city people and to prove their point, they criticize the people living in the countryside, like for example the people of the northern and southern parts of Holland, who are stamped as countryside people. Normally the impression is that the people living in the towns and the villages are more religious and of course they will say that they are more humane than those people living in the cities, who have the normal excuse that they are always very busy. The people of Zaandam are quite influenced by the Amsterdamers and are adopting their ways and style of living. No matter whether they like it or not or even want to adopt it or not, they are still searching. Perhaps they wanted their place to be internationally famous as well and that is their right too. No doubt the Netherlands is one of the liberal European countries and one can find many liberal factors of life in the vicinity of Amsterdam, perhaps that is why the Zaanstad people feel compelled to adopt a few things from the liberal culture of Amsterdam.

I know that liberalism and humanism are two quite different words having two different concepts. Liberty is a positive factor and should be part of any human life but to some extent. I have always maintained that there should be some measure on liberty and definitely a limit to it. That is not so in the Western world which is then the cause of mismanagement hence resulting in churches being converted to discos and clubs. This is so because the people are not getting their peace from churches and are then changing their priorities. Religion for them has changed to a disco and club going life. But neither is that giving them any peace.

Certainly they think that the disco life is highly enjoyable and thus they are searching and exploring some aspects of life no matter whether it is time or not. I have been there for the sole purpose to get more information about the disco people and their thinking. By saying the disco people I would rather say the people who entered the discos for specific reasons and intentions. I have thus been to the discos in different countries where I have met people from different cultures and who have different schools of thought. I have also talked to the people belonging to different age groups to get to know their point of view and about their life. None of them really had convincing arguments and points. I got the impression that they were frustrated and went to discos to get out their frustration but I am afraid to say that they came back with even bigger frustration. Thus, that is how the circle of life is going on for them, and I have seen all these people somehow keeping up this pattern of life.

To me this shows how far they are from the spiritual quality of life which certainly is necessary for peace of mind. They need to develop the spiritual aspect of life and also to promote it in the young generation which is going further and further astray. Also, then we would be able to avoid big disasters which occur in the shape of wars for power, the conversion of mosques to temples and churches to discos. I would request the religious leaders and priests of all the existing religions to start thinking about these major problems and plan for a convenient solution for the peace of the people and this world. They should start by improving themselves by making themselves practical examples for other people to follow, instead of trying to correct the others and not improving themselves first.

WHAT A CONTRAST

In every part of the world we have seen that just an ordinary person has done some spectacular work for the society and then become a model for others. One such humanist is a British lady whom I am going to write about. Britian is a part of this human world and there are many philanthropists and talented people there. Though one may be at variance with the ideology and culture of the British the talent and humanity found there cannot be ignored, and other factors which show or promote prejudice can be ignored in cases where more good than negative values can be found.

In this world where there is a lot of violence and hatred going on; where there is fighting to prove the superiority of certain countries over others and there is a lot of propaganda to ridicule the differences of life, culture and especially religion; a lot of good people exist as well. These people care for others and are working for the sake of humanity voluntarily. For them it is not necessary to know people to help them, it is enough that others are human beings with the same feelings and desires as they have. They have an unselfish spirit which has filled them up with love and devotion to mankind. We should always be proud of such people and promote this divine quality in the world.

The lady whom I have chosen to write about is helping humanity in a way quite apart from the others. Now, this might not be as interesting or as important to other people as it is for me. What the lady does is to write letters to the prisoners - yes, to those unfortunate people who have been involved in criminal activities. She writes particularly to those prisoners who have death sentences. These people are destined to die for their illegal activities and for this reason mostly the religious groups ignore them since they are a bad investment; I have had to use these words because that is the real fact. But she was very optimistic and she thought that she could help them. Of course she was sure that she can not change the history or she can not help them to be released from their prisons but her intentions were to help others through helping these prisoners.

She was a genius and wanted to communicate with the next generation by letting society know those reasons which make a normal human being a criminal, whether these people who had committed crimes were really bad or had committed crime only because of bad personality traits. She wanted to make the prisoners realize as well that due to their crimes all their loved ones and their families were suffering and they had been a bad influence on society. So she was actually killing two birds with one stone in her way. It was quite a hard task but her strong will and determination made her to go on and help the needy since she believed that the behaviors of the people can be improved and she condemned the statement that, 'once a thief always a thief'.

According to her point of view there are many ways to improve the situation, while its easy to snub and criticize people we have a choice, we can understand that the criminal activities of these people are a cry for help. They had always felt neglected by one way or another. That is why it is always good to sympathize with them for if they were not needy then why were they asking for help and why had they done what was not normal? In fact most of them are asking for help and because of their false images and pride they cannot reveal this characteristic in the normal way. In any situation they are not strong people and are hiding behind their cowardice.

This is happening in every country and a lot of examples can be taken from the lady's own country. Usually prisoners never get proper treatment from society and religious groups. It is the general impression that people are hostile towards them, particularly in the Eastern world and even in the East European countries and the prisoners are being treated sub-standard. According to the official figures crime rates are higher in those places where even the punishments are more severe. That clearly seconds the idea of my respected lady. That could be a reason when once one commits a crime, one tries continue to do so on since one has noticed that in most circumstances society will keep blaming no matter whatever one will do, and that can be very discouraging. Definitely we do not need to mingle with criminals but on the other hand we do not have treat them as outcasts. We have to arrange some seminars or training programmes for people who want help and we have to encourage those who want to get out from that circle so that more and more people can try to improve upon their past mistakes.

I know a few religious organizations are working to help prisoners. One religious group helping prisoners to reform is the Jehovah group who are yet trying to be fully recognized in society, as their position is rather ambiguous. Different people have different opinion about them, I know most of the people in the Western world who do not even allow the people belonging to this group to talk with them. Why! Maybe because of their style of preaching or otherwise. I am not canvassing any religious thoughts but I would certainly say if any one or any group, no matter whether we like it or not is working for the sake of humanity then we should not stop them as we have no right to act as God. Let us leave God's job to God.

The good lady is of the view that though these people are criminals and have been involved in crime, there could be a big possibility that they have committed crimes under some stress and due to improper conditions and their sad backgrounds. She feels that they do acknowledge their negative activities and are remorseful. Thus there should be a person open enough to befriend them for the sake of humanity and try to help them to rehabilitate. She consciously believes that this is her duty and purpose in life. Her very strong belief is the need to control crime for the good of the society. But the only way is not to convict people. According to her we should try to have some sort of social contact with these people in the hope of helping them to convert to the normal way of life, the main reason of which is to make our society better. The better solution, for her, is to save life rather than to destroy it.

I am sure the Saudi's and the Arabs will not be impressed with her ideas. But on the other hand, as one wise person said we have to consider what is being said rather than to consider who said it. Therefore they should not consider the nationality of the lady, they have to see if the idea appeals to them there is still time for them to have some reasonable improvement in their constitutions, since it is never too late.

I believe in this pious lady and her approach of life. Hence I wanted to convey her message to everyone. Hopefully we will think about this aspect and may create an amiable environment around us and certainly we might try to solve the problem rather than to squash it. Since the more reality is hidden, the more exposed it is, and it has been proven according to Newton's one law of motion as well. If we do this, we would in fact be promoting this problem and negative values rather than to find the appropriate solution to reduce it. Thus we need a lot of these ladies to promote this good cause in this world rather than to keep hush and let anarchy take over in the world and snub and destroy the innocent and good people on this earth.

SENSE OF RESPONSIBILITY

THIS BOOK IS CONCERNED MAINLY with the cultural aspect of life and the major problems confronting the two different cultures - Eastern and Western. I felt very privileged and lucky that I got the opportunity to have contact with different sorts of people from different fields of life. I have also observed youth of both sides and studied their opinion about responsibility and why and how they feel the sense of responsibility. Also, what is the major factor which compels them to be fully responsible in everything that they do. Is it because they have to and have no choice and no way out, or they can not escape it due to their cultural backgrounds which has imposed on them the sense of responsibility. Here, the two different types should be mentioned so that the difference can be known.

As I have already mentioned a lot of people from the Eastern world are entering into Western countries to work, but their ideology is not to work for amassing extra fortunes and buy mansions, but to work for their families back home to fulfill their necessities of life like food, shelter, clothing and education. They, thus have huge responsibilities on their shoulders in the shape of their immediate families and are devoting themselves to save these lives. In the normal family system of the Eastern part, the elders of the families work hard to support and look after the younger family members. They want to do so to prove their responsibility for their family and through that to show their love and affection, as family values and ties in the Eastern culture are quite different from the Western culture. The cultural ties are too strong, if one wants to escape from them, one simply cannot since there is a big check on every action. If one will keep going on against the cultural values there are strong chances that one will be outcast by one's own loved ones and family. One can clearly feel that there is some sort of psychological blackmail existing in that culture.

In contrast, in the Western culture there are a mixture of policies, which compel the young people to live with their parents only till a certain age. They thus do show to the other part of the world that their young generations are more equipped and much more liberal. It is quite evident that the young of the Western world have more exposure and know how than the other parts of the world, which is simply because of the awareness and this does not mean they are better than other. Their intentions and the ideas are very positive but in reality it has different impacts as well. They have to even maintain policies to retain the young people in the home boundaries; that is the big difference of thought and culture. In the Western families the normal trend for the teenagers is that the moment they get the chance to live on their own they leave their parents, and in some cases even before the official age of achieving liberty for their actions. We all know that there are exceptions and in this case the possibility of exceptions is on the increase. There are many factors which prompt such thinking in the young minds such as their up bringing since one way or another they are not happy with the way of life. That is why we have a big contrast between the two cultures.

On one hand, one type is trying to take too much responsibility and care of their family and on the other hand, the other type wants to get out of the situation as quickly as possible. What they do not realize is that it is all a matter of love, care and devotion - the most inherent feeling of a human being for his loved one - and the more the elders realize this fact of life, the more satisfactory and positive result they can get. To keep children at home by force is not the solution and nor is it to send children abroad or outside their homes.

Everyone has got to realize their duty towards each other and themselves so that one does not get more burden than one can bear. Otherwise the extra burden one will transfer to others and the more problems everyone will face. Nowadays we are facing a big problem of how to handle our teenagers and how to bring up a child in this world. It really does not matter whether it is East or West, every one has these problems. The intensity and the ratio could be different but the problem is for the whole world.

The young generation is starting to tell their elders that this is the nineties, which partly they have learned from their elders and they are trying to communicate to their elders to please grow up. It looks really very amazing but what I do not understand is why the elders get upset for they might have done the same with their elders as well. They will realize this if they are sincere and honest with themselves. It looks as if this will go on until unless we start trying from today to watch our behavior before making the decision on whether we need a child or not, and everyone has to be responsible for their actions. We have to be sure of the kind of world we want to give to our children or are we just making this decision for the sake of the decision; like most of the people get married because they like or love to be a bride or a bridegroom. To be a bride or a bridegroom might be easy but to prove it or justify the position is entirely another case. We should at least have to make certain standards in society before bringing our children in this world rather than to ask the community or society to do something.

The moment we let anyone else solve our problems there is a good chance that we will not get satisfactory results, and if we do not get the satisfaction we will not be content and without contentment there is no fun in life, which has been proven time and time again. Therefore there will always be a good chance of discrepancy somewhere and somehow. It is just like if two people are quarreling it is easier to solve their problem rather than that of more people quarreling with each other at the same time. Then it would really be a mess and would be hard to find out the cause of the quarrel since the more people will talk, the more complexity will be created and nobody would really like to be a part of the messy situation. What is happening is we have created so much confusion that we do not really know anymore what is right and wrong. Most of the time we are spending our positive energies for nothing.

Also it would be healthy for the elders as well in their old age to get the same love, care and devotion from their offspring's as they had earlier showed them. It is only possible if they perform their duties the way they are supposed to. Their children would then think twice of sending their old parents to the rotten nursing homes. I am not against the nursing homes, I really appreciate the idea and the people working there who are taking care of old people and showing their love and affection to them which they might have not receive from their own families and loved ones. That shows them to be very humane. But this idea really works effectively only in some situations, but when we start considering this as a system, then I am against it. It looks like there is a gap somewhere somehow.

Be careful since 'what goes around comes around'; this does explain many factors of life depending on how one looks at this theory. The people who do not know, I would call them to take note as it is for them a better time to acquire this knowledge. And the people who are all too aware, should start implementing it in their lives. The more we are polite, generous, affectionate and humble with our dependents then surely the more we will get the same positive result back in our old age and this would certainly save our society from deteriorating. It has been proven that normally people are trying to give their best to others if they get the feeling that the other person is sincere with them. Therefore if the child and the parents develop a bond with which they are comfortable, we shall soon see a change for the better.

MISERABLE LIBERTY

WHENEVER WE THINK ABOUT THE religion in the Western world, the first thing that comes to our mind is Christianity since most of the Western parts are influenced by Christianity. We know that, not every part of the world is Christian but the system is influenced by it directly or indirectly. In the same way most of the Eastern part has the influence of Islam and also Buddhism can be seen there. Actually the point of discussion is how the Muslims are living in the East and the Christians in the West, and how safe they are there. How are the two cultures protecting their respective people with their competitive policies.

The word competitive has been deliberately used as these two major religions of the world are always working hard to prove their supremacy over each other. One can say they are working in the true marketing style. In a market one has to sell one's goods in any way possible since there are no fixed patterns and one can always alter the rules and regulations depending on the competition. In this way these two religious groups are in the world open market and are, by one way or another trying to attract people, but have little least concern for the improvement of the people. Though they claim that they are working for the sake of humanity, and their respective religions taught them to love and care for everyone, practically they are forming policies for their own interests.

I was reading a survey report regarding the youngsters living in U.S.A and England. A group of students made a very important survey about the number of rapes going on. One in five people would definitely have undergone this abuse. Now how can these people trust and love other human beings when they have not received their share from the society. Definitely they will carry hostility towards other human beings and it would be very hard for them release the past and start living a normal life. Is it one of the reasons why in the Western world it is becoming normal not to trust in relationships? Everyone is scared from inside and nobody wants to be a victim, that is why they have started campaigning that blood is thicker than water, which means men and women can come and go but the relatives will remain relatives. There was a time when the society was teaching everyone to respect husband or wife but nowadays we are living in the world where these things do not really matter. Then what are we complaining about? In one way we are communicating the message which is definitely promoting the concept of mistrust and in the same way we want to defend the divorce rates. First we need to work within ourselves and we have to come out from this double standard status so that we can help ourselves. The question is who to blame and in some cases how to blame. Would the blame be fully on the culture or on the society?

Most young people do not know the limits and are exploring everything themselves. For them there is no limit on any kind of activity and again it is human nature to try to do better than the others and do everything as early as possible. Thus all limits are being crossed. Certainly it is getting harder and harder to distinguish between evil and good nowadays. No one really seems to me in a position to tell these youngsters what to do, because in most cases their own elders were in the same positions one way or another and it is hard for them to convince their youngsters not to make those mistakes which they have made. Would they listen and are they listening? If not then what is the remedy? Well, in the general situation what we have seen is that people experiment and others learn out of their experiences. But then a certain point comes where everyone acknowledges the theory and starts practicing and implementing it in the practical world. That is one of the reasons that nowadays the world has too many facilities which our ancestors did not have. We have benefited from the efforts of the past.

Without rules of the road the accident rate would be higher. Rules have thus been set up to control the number of accidents and ensure the safety and security of life. So do we not have to think about introducing certain rules in society so that no one would exceed the limits! It is just like a person who drinks beyond his limits and starts thinking that he is the lord of the world. Which I am afraid is happening around us and daily we hear a lot of news about drunk drivers and drunk people. They are causing much trouble for us but still nobody has really decided to ban alcohol particularly for drivers. Every time we make new policies on how to control drunk drivers and every time the results are the same since it is impossible to tell people what is their limit with regard to drinking.

Do we not think it is time for us to make a rule for ourselves and for our coming generations that alcohol is not allowed for drivers so that we can save countless lives and also control a big social problem? It is not the fault of alcohol but it is a matter of the education which one receives in one's early years and how one applies it in one's life. What we see in all these cases is indeed too much liberty somewhere somehow. Now what really bothers me is when I hear from my friends that limitations are not good and create more curiosity and urge us to commit more crimes. I would say, I do understand that people should not be restricted to cages but at the same time we should have to make a certain plan for ourselves and for our society on how we really want our lifestyle to be. In most parts of the Western world the people are so organized and logical that it makes me admire them but at the same time a thought comes to my mind, that these people who have made the world so great and powerful could not find proper ways to solve their problems and straighten up their own lives.

Among the Western people the Irish have some control over themselves and still believe in some sort of family values. But to the others they are rated as third-class and their beliefs are considered fanatical and conservative whereas they believe they have more strong family and cultural values than other West European countries. What about the so-called liberal people who are trying to make life easier and are trying to facilitate people. Is this the definition of liberty or is this system making life more prosperous. If not then why can't we modify or improve this system which is killing people morally and socially and that is worse than any kind of murder. This is not the killing of one group of people but it involves a whole generation. The culprits deserve some sort of punishment which is quite hard to determine.

In the Eastern countries the problems are different, rape does occur there as well but the proportion is low as compared to their counterpart countries. But over there it is the morals of the people which are being played with in the other way around. The people's basic rights of life are being denied. A group of people are using their authority to force the other people to adopt the ideologies they believe in. Whenever force is used there is always a great chance of rebellion and this is why most of the youngsters are victims of insecurity and dissatisfaction. The people are least concerned with altering some of the rules and this is the main cause of the rebellion of the youth in these countries. It is imperative to provide security and responsibility so that the increasing negative values can be curbed as much as possible and the future can be secured.

This is the main reason why I always maintain that my religion is humanity, since to me this is more important than any other official label. All the holy books preach the same message - humanity and peace - and therefore the basics of all the religions convey the same meaning, but they have different ways of practice. The word religion has a very strong meaning and is all-important. The moment a person shows that he believes deeply in his religion, the attitude of the people changes and this is the big question for the religious followers. I am proud of all religions and their theories when the people practice them fairly and do not manipulate according to their own interests. The young generation needs a lot of study and personal observation. This is necessary since traditions usually give a negative impression to them. We should make our life disciplined to get the proper feedback from the system we belong to. Also change is needed for the peace and security of the people, not only for one particular system but for all cultures. If we misuse values then we certainly would lose and bury the culture. Of course we need to save our cultural background but at the same we need to help and facilitate our youngsters as well.

ANOTHER PHASE OF LIBERTY

I

WHILE ON THE TOPIC OF liberty a few points must be mentioned in detail which while they disturb many of us, on the other hand could appeal to some people. To talk about what is attractive is quite difficult and is itself a large topic, for every person has his or her own way of thinking and opinion according to which everyone determines their own life and does not go beyond a certain limit.

Well, a phase which is really perturbing and confusing is the peculiar relationship of a mother and daughter. Peculiar in the sense that they have a complete life-style of their own and do not welcome any sort of interference from any other person and have crossed all the boundaries of the relationship. They have full satisfaction and enjoyment by themselves and they really have their own unique way. Of course every person is trying or would like to have complete enjoyment by oneself, but this mother and daughter relationship is really special. They do not even want anyone to disturb the 'purity' of their relationship. They keep themselves for each other in every way and when I say every way that means infect every way. If any third person even touches either of them, their reaction is rigid and severe. Such is their attachment to each other, that no person can have a physical relationship with either of them.

We know it is the right of every person to obtain their satisfaction in life through the way they want and I am the first person who would encourage people to get their happiness in their own way. But at the same time we should always consider the moral and sexual limits so that we should not initiate any destructive force in the society. When I think on this particular issue my mind forces me to ask whether is it affection or possession? At the same time I am not avoiding the fact that perhaps they are suffering some kind of sickness! By the way, where does the motherly bond and respect go? The word mother itself sounds very safe and sacred to most of us. However when it is being used in this way, people will soon be suspicious about so many mothers and that is not good in any circumstances. Or are we just experimenting like in so many other cases? Is it a part of our creative work as well?

If our own mothers, teachers or the leaders of the society have a dubious character then how can we expect any kind of guidance from them? In these kind of cases we face more problems since there is a lot of ambiguity involved and usually we cannot figure out the case in the right time. It is a time-taking process and a lot of keen observation is needed to find the nuances in these kinds of difficult cases and to be sure it. It is only then that any solution can be thought of to save these cases. These cases are often very sneaky and mostly cowardice is involved since no one comes up with the skeletons in their closets. Let us say 'God bless them', for we should show our positive characters to them and then let them do what they want. Maybe, by keeping our solid characters we could help those people who yet have to come out of their closets and change their thoughts. It is a natural phenomenon for people to be impressed with each other, though it is very difficult to say which habits or ways can alter the thoughts of the people. We really need to point out these 'special' people with no delay before we will be forced to accept them as a part of our normal societies. I have no doubt that most of us are clearly aware of the pros and cons.

II

Whenever Eastern people hear about the Western culture and its main feature liberalism, their first reaction is to be impressed and attracted to it. But lets talk about the people who live there and what are really their thoughts and opinions. Are they really happy people? Does the definition of happiness which exist in most of the Eastern parts means anything to them? I did a small scale survey as to why other people were attracted towards the culture of the Western people. Naturally I have received very different answers and the main answer which I got was that Westerners do not think that they have as such extra liberty. For them all the facilities that they have in their lives are very normal and they think that most of them are the basic necessities of anyone's life. The feelings of non-satisfaction in life exists in the Western parts as well and they are facing as much problems in life as any other part of the world. The only difference could be the nature of the problems, but life is not as easy as it has been portrayed in most of the Eastern world. Awareness and the education, I believe are very good but sometimes one can sense, to know too much can be a big problem in some situations. Perhaps cloning could be the relevant example in this situation?

The cultural thing to explore the world and to know everything and try to reach God can make the people find God, but then we do not have to forget our holy books. According to the Holy Quran and the Holy Bible, a time will come when mankind will reach their utmost and their satanic abilities will be more prominent then ever. Sometimes a flicker of doubt comes in my mind to say are we facing that time? People now want to conquer all the mysteries of the universe and of the divine nature as well and are now even trying to analyze their own Resurrection. Certainly, different names are given to all these aspects - experiments, practical, therapy etc etc. Despite the fact that the people are laughing about the idea of Doomsday, if it really happens and if all the indications which are given in the respective holy books are right, then where are we standing! Now since it is inevitable that there is a super power which is beyond the reach of human beings do we not have to think twice before involving ourselves into this technological rather mechanical world? Do we not need to keep intact our respective ethics which we have learned through our books? We should not close these books since we are not yet clear about our new ways which everyone has chosen for their own convenience.

What do these words really mean? Let us talk about therapy only. What does therapy really mean and why do we really need therapy in our lives or is it a self-created problem? These are the few possible questions which one can raise all the time. In the Western culture the trend is to know everything possible about your own life from childhood. It sounds very interesting but as a matter of fact it is a very painful experience which one would like to have in life. That is to say, were they really abused in any way and if so how much and was it moral, sexual or any other sort of abuse. To my knowledge, which I got first hand from them, a large majority of the people in one way or the other come to know that their own parents, uncles, aunties and even their own brothers and sisters abused them in the early years of their childhood.

Now in the other parts of the world this kind of therapy cannot even be thought about and in many cases they cannot even afford it, but it is very normal and common in the Western world. I do not mean by saying that since in the Eastern world these kinds of therapies are not common that is why the child abuse is not there. Of course it exists over there but entirely in different ways. Young children have to work and in some cases they have to earn money for their parents and for their other family members, and in some parts parents even sell their children just to make ends meet. I wonder why people are use the young generation and play with their feelings and then keep saying that they have not done anything wrong for them. It makes me to think how can these people convince themselves and what about their conscience? How can they keep telling themselves that they are not wrong. These are the valid problems for both the cultures no matter whether it is East or West. That could be the reason that people from both the cultures are frustrated and when they do not find those factors in their own cultures they start appreciating the other and try to escape from their own realities. But we have to be sure the solution is not always to escape from the situation, sometimes it is better to stick with the problem and find the positive remedy. Are we not looking for this in both cultures?

Another major problem is the people who have been through all the therapy business including undergoing treatment by the clairvoyant and participating in séances as well. Sometimes they become psycho-patients in one way or the other and feel themselves to be even more misfit and left-out in the society and they then bear more grudges against their families and relatives. So the sufferer keep suffering and the funny thing is in many cases they are facing more problems after the professional help.

Now how much truth is involved in therapy treatment; I had better not deal with this as this is entirely the therapist's job and I leave it to them, but I can observe the side-effects of this therapy and the bad influences on society. It is certainly due to this kind of therapy treatment that relationships are adversely effected. It is one of the reasons that the divorce rates are on the increase and ultimately it is creating more problems for the children. In some of these cases the relevant authorities often rule that these parents are not eligible to take proper care of their own children. Thus, the therapy which they had thought to be the solution, creates yet more serious problems. They had thought that they would come to know all their problems and be free from them. But the consequences have quite an opposite effect on their lives. Hence these types of people and parents keep on having a series of never-ending problems.

They are totally consumed by curiosity to know about themselves and this is indeed human nature as well. I still believe therapy is a good facility, in some cases people are unable to solve their own problems but since they are not really major problems the therapist can guide them through. In most cases there is no need to delve into the past at all. But what I do not understand about the treatment is that there is no point to air anyone's dirty laundry if it is not really necessary. We know everyone has something missing in their lives, that is why some of them consult the therapist but this does not mean that they should play with humanity as seems to be happening in many cases nowadays. As a matter of fact it should be the duty of any professional therapist to help everyone and try to stop the trend in people to know about their dead past.

Lots of people have sessions with the astrologers and palmists to know their past and future. To go for therapy is one of the modern approach of life and people always believe it is totally for their own good and there can be no negative effects. Astrology and palmistry are also quite in fashion, and there are a lot of books on these topics but the people's reaction is to be merely amused by these kinds of books. They seems to believe firmly in therapy and find it more convincing than palmistry or astrology.

Though the people are really sure of the therapy, my question is do we really need therapy? Are we now so insecure about our lives and our elders or is it the case that all the children now undergo abuse? If our answer is positive for all of these questions, then we can say we do desperately need therapy. But, with the observation of my colleagues as well, I think this is not really the truth. Yes, crimes do occur but not as much as the media is indicating. It is the propaganda of the media not to let both cultures know about the realities and their main policy seems to be to divide them and rule. We can always ignore the bad egg but it is a pity that though we are aware of what is good and bad, we have become so insecure and indecisive that it has become a part of the problem. It is certainly always good to know about the past and learn from the mistakes so that we do not have to repeat them. At the same time we have to closely look at our future and prepare for it as well. If knowing more about the past creates trouble for our future, then there is no meaning in knowing those faults which bring more disastrous effect for our future.

LIFE SACRIFICE

ONE OF THE MOST POPULAR and festive day in Holland is the Carnival day with everyone looking forward to 'partying' on this day, or rather freaking-out. There must be a lot of people in the Eastern part perhaps who do not know the importance of this day. On this day, people dress up in different kinds of costumes, mostly of different animals. One can be anything one wants, and can imitate any animal which gives inspiration to them. Yes, one can be a horse, cow, pig and certainly they can always try to be a 'B' and the son of a 'B' as well. The importance of this day serves these people very well for they have the freedom to wear any sort of costume and impersonate any other living thing which fascinates them.

The amazing fact is, the people who act in normal life in a bitchy way can also be dressed up in their true costumes, but ironically their costumes still hide their original characters. Thus, these people are very well covered-up and protected by their costumes. In addition to their disguise they get full applause and encouragement for parading themselves, since no one wants to lose this tradition and the tabloids keep covering these kinds of events in a very sensational way. Therefore the people keep on making this day an important event in their lives. People will go on covering themselves up and not show their true characters but in some cases, people will be showing their true selves through the costumes they have chosen to wear. Such is the great truth and irony of this day. Of course people would have difficulties to get at the bottom of these people, other nasty types wear costume as a cover up and could also wear 'B' costume. But the pity here is that to be a 'B' one has to spend money to buy the costumes. I mean, people have to spend an amount of their money to get this character. Those who want to be like that, do bear the expenses only to get that label in the honorable way. So, they are squandering away their wealth only to show their true selves through the costumes they choose. Sometimes it sounds so good to me that life is so easy in so many ways, if we somehow manage to celebrate more days like a carnival day then we can very easily hide our characters and perhaps escape from the harsh realities. To me this seems a very nice way of meditation.

But on the other hand, all these people are always talking about the developing countries and the serious problems of the people over there, like in the different African and Asian countries. They show concern for the truly needy people over there and go through all the feelings and emotions of grief. Yet, they prefer to spend their money on looking like animals, rather than putting the money to true and genuine use. They ignore them after paying lip-service to them, and prefer to squander their wealth only for a few minutes of satisfaction and pleasure. Yes they do need their satisfaction, but at the same time they should realize, even only for a minute, that a few pennies can change the lives and careers of other people. Instead of finding pleasure in imitating and prancing about like animals, would it not be better in every way to be helpful for our fellow human beings? Rather than checking our human qualities and putting our energies in finding which animal has more influence on us, is it not better to stick to our own kind and find out more about human qualities?

Human beings are indeed part of the animal kingdom, but are endowed with civilized qualities and when I talk about civilization, I am sure that all the Dutch know the meaning of this word for they are always in search of ways to make the system better and establish more positive rules and regulations. Though English is not the first language of the Dutch they do have sufficient knowledge of the language to understand very well the meaning of the word civilization. This is one of the major reasons why I like the Dutch, for they do not hesitate to talk in any foreign language which they are familiar with. Certainly they are far better than the other fellow European countries where people are deliberately reluctant to talk in any other language than their own.

It was not my main intention to criticize the carnival day or the Dutch people, but to write about some sudden news I had heard on this day. Usually when I am at home, all my friends call me as they know I am living alone and far away from my family, and they always try their best to fill this gap. I feel very blessed that I have a few good people around me and that is their contribution in my life that I enjoy living everywhere. On one such day, one of my friends called me to give me some important news which was being telecasted. It was an interview of a young lady who worked for the Playboy magazine. She was a French-born American and the most important point of her session was for me a very liberal thought which she made clear through her own limits of judgment. She very seriously and bluntly said that she wanted to make her own contribution to society, and that was for her to show her body to the public and society. Thus her purpose of living, according to her, was not for herself but for others. From her style of explaining herself and her facial expression I could not really figure out what she meant by her point of view. It was a wonderful fact that she wanted to contribute to society, but the way she had adopted repelled me. For me it was quite complicated to figure out her intentions. Being an optimistic person I certainly do not doubt her wishes, but I would doubt that she did not have any other skills or maybe she had failed somewhere in life due to which she had lost her potential. But even then she had retained the spirit to keep going on and do something for the people and that is why she had devoted herself to this profession.

I feel very sorry for this young lady, that she has to exhibit herself just to reach her goal. I am sure there must be so many other ways perhaps more suitable for her to contribute herself the society, but she had personally chosen that way. I really have heard in different parts of the world people are selling their bodies or showing themselves to the public, but the main reasons which I have heard is that mostly they wanted to pay their bills and they have to do all this for their own selves and in some cases for their families' survival. But the way she had chosen to execute her aim made really impressed and astonished me as well.

At the same time I feel proud of the thought which made her to choose the life-style of contributing herself to people. To me it does not matter what she does but what really matters is her intentions and feelings for other human beings. It is the usual style of people to call people such as this girl sluts, prostitutes etc. People do not have to deny this label which they have allocated to these kinds of people, but they have to consider that they are also human beings and there is no one who is better or worse in this world. What I do not understand is how can people blame these girls that they are not good human beings whereas they are the ones who visit them quite frequently. If blame is attributable to anyone, it is to those who visit these girls.

If these girls are so bad, then how come in every part of the world every year people are spending millions for Playboy magazines and for x-rated movies. Are we not living with terrible sorts of double standards, and how long can we go on living with this denial? We are nobody to love and hate someone due to what they do or they have done, but we are responsible for our own actions. Perhaps now is the time to consider our own actions and how we can implore and help others.

UNION IS STRENGTH

SINCE THE MUSLIM MOTTO IS "one" and strength in unity then its surprising that they cannot effect leadership for the world instead of depending on the other superpowers of the world? This is indeed the thought of the Christians and the people belonging to the other respective religions. Not even one Muslim land or country is self-supporting and is not in need of aid from the Western countries. This is the main question of most of the Western people. When I also became aware of this attitude of the Westerners about the situation in the East, I thought a lot about this matter and started asking myself - why?

I have come across many Muslims from different countries and its clear that while they all have the same religion - Islam - yet their basics are quite different from each other. They condemn and differ with each other in the race to show their supremacy over each other; rather than to be an example of unity and peace to the rest of the world and show the true concept of Islam which literally means 'submission' - to God.

Another fact is that if people live in their own homelands they practice religion in a different way, and the moment they start living in other countries they reveal themselves in a very different way and explain religion according to their own convenience and that definitely creates problems for the beginners to understand. I came to know about a group called 'Elevi' originating in Turkey. Their most conspicuous point is that there is no belief in praying like all the other Muslims do. According to them, Imam Hussein died during prayer and since they call themselves his followers, they have rejected the act of praying and thus do not go to mosques. The surprising point is this group is a part of the Shiite sect who do believe in praying.

On the other hand, some of the Iranians rarely believe in the two important festivals of Islam - Eid-ul-Fitr and Eid-ul-Adha in lieu of which they have their own traditional festivals. Their calendar differs from the others and has a different new year. These are some of the main facts which compel the other people of the world not to take Islam seriously. It is no wonder when they see so much confusion and hatred amongst the Muslims and they have therefore decided that there is no point to know and understand this religion. Whereas, to the best of my knowledge the basics of Islam is peace, stability and love for all hatred for none. We know it is inherent human nature to go for relaxing and acceptable situations so people do not even bother to show keen interest in acquainting themselves with the real fundamentals of Islam. It is also due to such created confusions in all the other religions as well that people are going astray from the religious life. Let us presume that if Islam is the complete religion then the Muslims' position should be very exemplary for the whole world. But in reality the picture is quite the opposite, especially nowadays. Almost everywhere in the Islamic world life is very insecure and unpredictable.

A further example is that of Ramadan - the sacred month of fasting in Islam. All the world is aware of this holy month. The concept of fasting is to know how life is for poor people when they do not have enough to eat and how do they survive in that particular situation. It was introduced only to minimize the differences between the poor and rich so that the people can be more loving and caring for each other. Now what is happening is different sects of Islam have their own way to select the start of this month and they have therefore dispersed the basic idea of unity. Well, it can be understandable in the case of different countries with different geographical locations, as the starting point of this month mainly depends upon the sighting of the moon and naturally that can vary in the different countries around the world. The difference then could be of one or two days, and should not be more than that.

But within one country the different groups select their own days though they could be in a same neighborhood! This is certainly beyond the knowledge of rational people and it does sound quite ridiculous as there is only one existing rule for the starting of Ramadan. O.k. in the Third world countries, the plea could be that of unresourcefulness and the sighting of the moon then depends on the naked eye. But what about the Western world where technology is at its height, where such differences are occurring as well. Is that fair for the other people to understand the religion? And how can the religious lords justify this?

All these points and realities do render me answerless for no one can deny them. I once heard an interview on the Dutch television of a writer who had declared in his book that, after a span of fifty years all the European countries would be converted into Islamic countries. It may sound very optimistic and I do appreciate the thought and the emotions of this writer, but I am afraid these feelings would not be helpful for him in any way. What he needs is to live in the practical world. We do not have to believe in such fantasies as these. As a matter of fact all they do is create more opposition and more hatred. Since people around the world see that in the Muslim world people live very traumatic lives they do not want to disturb their own peace. Of course this statement would be more effective if life were more secure in the Muslims countries and people would be automatically bound to listen to such ideas for their own prosperity, practically this should be the case but it is happening otherwise. I would therefore request my superiors who are in the position to convey their messages to discuss this important matter regarding the reality and the statistics, and they should be more practical and productive rather than live in fantasies and to give fantastical statements.

I feel the need to write another incident regarding the impression of Islam in the Western world. It is a true incident which took place in the Netherlands and made front page news in the daily Telegraph. Two asylum-seekers from Somalia had been sent to an asylum center where they were given a room with two beds and attached bath and kitchen. But they refused to live in such a place where they had to do all the cooking by themselves. According to them it was against the rule of Islam for men to cook! In their own countries it was the women folk who did all the cooking and the men folk never did any cooking in their lives nor intended to. Their reaction was to throw furniture about and break down the place. Imagine, this is the impression Muslims are giving to those people who already condemn them and their culture. The real concept and the basis of Islam has not yet been introduced to them. They have only seen what the so-called Muslims are showing them and are not fully aware of the real Islam. Even then, they are behaving very nicely with the Muslims but I think it is time for Muslims to think what they are communicating to the rest of the world, and is this really the concept of religion?

Furthermore those cultures in which Islam has a very quaint and difficult meaning show more hatred against Islam when they come across such situations and statements, whereas the facts are quite different and the real meaning and practice of Islam is quite the opposite. It is very normal for anyone to use the art of lying to capture one's interest and it is acceptable in a few cases, but it becomes a crime to use the platform of Islam or any other religion for petty matters. I do believe and it is clearly written in all the 'Traditions' that the Holy Prophet Mohammed (pbh) did all his chores and work by himself and was not dependent on anyone. All the Muslims believe in this fact which has been obviously stated in all the Islamic histories and other relevant books, then where does the rule spring from that cooking by men is forbidden? I would here mention that it is not normal in Christianity for the people to use the religious path for their personal excuses and if some of them do, then they are badly criticized as well. Therefore they are not accustomed to this sort of behavior and this is a big difference between the Western people and the Muslims' world. Of course not all the Westerners act like that, but the majority are free from these types of lame excuses.

WHAT ARE RIGHTS

I CAME TO KNOW ABOUT 'THE couple' who have been living together for the last four years. It was a relationship between two men living in the same place and sharing their lives in all aspects. I have to make it clear, not every part of the world where two men or two women are living together, means that they are having a relationship. It is mostly existing in the Western culture but again not in every situation. Therefore I am getting the privilege to call them a 'special couple', as they were gay as well. Of course I am not calling them special because they were gay but only because of their somehow exclusive human characteristics. Since I want to show the intensity of the relationship I see no point to ponder on the sexuality of the couple.

Aids, the deadly disease is on the increase in the world and we all know that most of the victims are homosexuals and bisexuals nowadays. After a year of the couple's relationship, one of them became a victim of the fatal disease which put an end to their physical relationship. Here I admire this decision of both of them and the fact that the other partner still carried on living with his companion as they saw no reason not to keep on living together. It is certainly a big sacrifice on anyone's part to live with an Aids patient as it is surely a deadly relationship and particularly when the relationship was only a year old. In such cases, usually people try to escape from the situation as it becomes quite difficult to cope. Human nature urges us to consider ourselves first and others next. But the couple decided to keep on living with the facts and did not want to leave each other simply because of sickness. This was for me a great surprise, as I have not seen many examples where people honor a one year relationship, particularly nowadays where dishonesty and cheating are a part of many stories.

It was therefore very admirable for the partner to keep on taking care of his mate for the next three years. Due to this relationship, he became an outcast and faced all sorts of problems including belonging to his church. His family had also rejected him for being a homosexual and for living with an Aids patient and he had been fired from at least three jobs due to the nature of his relationship. But here, look at the determination of the man to keep on living with his dying partner and caring for him. It had been a year that he was in this position and jobless, although he had had a solid career of ten years or so. But that was now all behind him due to his decision to nurse his sick partner.

It was around this time that I interviewed him on his choice of life. I am giving here the main points of our conversation. According to him, right from childhood he had never been attracted to the opposite gender and had never liked them. To him it was nothing to do with choice, but that was what it was. He had been afraid of society and its reaction and he had therefore kept this to himself and had tried to change himself. He even started living with a woman and tried his best to work out the relationship, but to no avail.

There was always a lack in physical relationship, but it was always the same and he was never really happy. He could not have a good relationship in this way and could not exchange his feelings and view of life and he felt that something was lacking in his relationships with women. We know a lot of men have these problems in their lives, and his explanation based on those facts which he elaborated to me, do not seem good enough reason to declare oneself gay. But anyhow, we know in former days and even today in many parts of the world, people do not accept these kinds of arguments and they clearly think that it is some kind of joke or sickness. I have even heard the Westerners describing it as some sort of insanity. Well I am not a judge, and certainly have no right to defend one and to oppose the other in this particular issue, but I have seen from my childhood and during my traveling, that there are few people who are completely different from others.

Now whether they have chosen that way themselves or they were naturally born that way, I cannot say. These people are being named very differently in different cultures. If they are born the way they are living their lives then we have no right to condemn and humiliate them, since God's love is for everyone and if God has made them the way they are then we are nobody to criticize their gender. But at the same time we hear nowadays quite often that people are declaring themselves to be gay or whatever, after spending part of their lives being 'straight' and in many cases they have children as well. These kinds of people force others to wonder that how come they are all of a sudden changing their personalities. Was there any sort of magic which changed them or were they having joke with the rest of the world? How can we define these particular situations? And is it lust? Because there are so many people who are coming out from their special closets, that is why it too difficult for the average normal human being to believe anyone of them.

Coming back to the partner explanation; after his disappointed experiences with women he then came across the guy who was now the Aids patient. It was with this guy that he felt he could communicate on all the things of the world and really find happiness and satisfaction in his life. Though they did not have any physical relationship anymore, they did think that they had a spiritual bond between them and that was what was keeping them together. The patient had not been quite mobile in the last two years and was almost confined to bed. His partner looked after him and nursed him, for to him this was his moral duty and from the point of view of humanity he felt that he had no right to leave a sick human being alone, knowing that such a person was in genuine need of a caring partner.

This ideology was so admirable it made me to forget that he had chosen a gay lifestyle. To me he was a great person, to transcend all the worldly qualities to come to the help of a sick human being. What else is humanity about? This also showed his unselfishness and genuine feelings for his partner. I certainly do not care what he did in his bedroom, but what I do consider is what I have seen for myself, and as we know actions speak louder than words. His practical approach made me think that he was not lying and he was a sincere human being, and to me that was itself great news since I have not seen many of these nowadays.

I do not like or hate homosexuals, but it was necessary for me to point out the credibility of any human being to learn more about life and humanity. And this has been my intention all along - to learn from this person and to show that God has given qualities to every single human being and we should know how to find out and how to learn and benefit from them. There are many ways to criticize people and reject them, but at the same time there are many ways to look for beauty so that the learning process keeps going on for the future generations. I believe a human being has no right to snatch other fellow human beings' basic rights of living. Are we not going too far?

REVENGE OR INTOLERANCE

THIS IS ABOUT A CHILD who was brought up in that part of the world where someone else was ruler. So right from childhood this child had personal liking and disliking for the ruler which kept developing with the passage of time. One thing he was sure from day-one was that his people were not capable of handling matters and that was why they were seeking help. Though he was against the ruling authorities, at the same time he kept hostility against his own people. As time went on, somehow the idea started building up in his mind that they were incompetent and he was spending his whole life in this confusion.

It was hard for him to blame anyone; sometimes he blamed the invaders and sometimes he blamed his own country fellows. He spent his sixty years trying to understand, but he could not find the right answer and attain his own peace. He kept asking this question quite often to himself, why were people being treated so differently, was it only because of their different color skin or because they were born in a certain part of the world? He could not get all his answers but what he understood was that he himself had started discriminating his own people and he reached a level where his own children started avoiding him. He knew he was wrong but he did not have the courage to accept it and as a matter of fact he did not have any other remedy for his children. The only thing that he knew was the bad influence which he got from his early childhood. Now who would take all the responsibility of this child's life? And who is to blame?

Actually this is the brief picture of a child's feelings and his story, who was born in 1920 and lived in the sub-continent under the British rule. His father worked for the British and traveled around the world with them and was eventually granted land from the British Empire. Though he had seen the land and had heard stories from his mother he did not have his own powerful memories of life with him. Perhaps his father was a very conventional sort of person who thought that his job was to earn money and be a provider while the mother role was to take care of the children. Whatever the reason, he did not have any strong memories about his father's life. Of course he loved his father and admired him as is the case with so many other children. But the real sad moment came with his father's sudden death when he was around the age of ten. He had been living a very nice life with his father and after his death there was nobody who seemed to care much. He faced many hardships in his life and he had to work hard to make ends meet.

He worked hard in his childhood and he kept studying as well. He had the motivation to prove himself and he had done all the things of the world to reach his target. Since he kept studying through all his bad and tough periods of life, now the time came when he was about to get the recognition of all his struggles. He passed his graduation examination and was awarded with a degree. For him at that time that degree was a piece of gold and it was to him like winning the lotto. It was for him his whole world at that time. He was very thrilled and happy to have worked so hard and he had reaped the reward from his God since he was a strong believer of God. By the way, what I learned from him and from his belief was that he had always been content even in the situation when things did not go according to his wishes. He believed even now that it was because of his strong belief and determination that he had made his life. He knew from day one that his life was not going to be simple and easy, but at the same time he knew there were so many people who had improved their lives due to their efforts and convictions, then why could not he.

After a span of hard life now it was the time for him to look for a job, a job which he had thought of in his early life. It did not take long to get a job with the British Army and he started working and living with them also. To be self-sufficient and independent meant a lot to him especially due to the early demise of his father. He felt very proud and obtained pleasure by helping his other family members as well. It was the cultural influence and part of his personality to be very loving with all his family members. He had both a brother and sisters, and half-brothers and half-sisters as well. Though he loved all of them, it happened to be his baby sister whom he dearly loved. She was the only sister younger than him before their father's death and they had shared many moments of their early childhood together. They could feel each other's pain and he felt subconsciously that he was responsible for her good future since in the sub-continent culture in those days women were very dependent and were not allowed to work freely. These circumstances exist very strongly even today. Though the values have changed and are still rapidly changing still one can see and feel that women are quite under the influence of men and in some cases they allow themselves to be dominated.

As he was working with the Army he had to move from one place to another since it was part of the rules and regulations of the Army not to live more than three years in one place. The personnel had to move everywhere around the country, and by the way that British rule is still applicable in the sub-continent. During his stay in another place, the other members of his family arranged the marriage of his baby sister and unfortunately he could not attend the marriage function. Though he was not a participant he was very happy for her since he thought he was responsible for her and now he felt relieved with the thought that she could live her own life. But when he came to know about his brother-in-law he was not happy due to the fact that the age difference was too great for he was almost double her age. He did not like that, but at the same time he do not want to lose contact with his sister. It took him a while to calm himself down and finally he wisely decided to accept the situation. Somehow he managed to work out a relationship with his brother-in-law, but infect psychologically he was never comfortable and happy with him and that was what he knew deep inside.

During his job he was earning quite a good amount and because he was single at that time, his brother-in-law advised him to save some amount for the future. In those days he had quite a frequent contact with him and this advice made sense to him as well. One day he came up with the idea to buy some properties to sell later on and in this way make some money for himself. The idea appealed to him but because of the nature of the job he had in those days he had the problem of managing it all by himself. His brother-in-law offered his co-operation to help him by buying the suitable properties for him. He now started counting on the same person, something which he had thought to be impossible for him. Because of his simple and gullible nature and honesty he soon started believing in his sincerity and that he would take good care for him. He made a deal with him and started sending money to him. His brother-in-law did manage to buy a few properties from his income. But what he did was to buy every single property in his own name. So this pattern went on, he never asked any proof from him and neither was he provided with any proof by him. It was simply and purely a blind confidence from each side. He was reluctant to ask any proof as he never even could imagine that his own family member would cheat him.

At this time in India major conflicts were cropping up between the Hindus and the Muslims. The Muslims were demanding a separate homeland where they could live according to their own religion and could practice more freely. To make a long story short, the partition of India and Pakistan occurred and thus both the Muslims and Hindus got their separate places. Mostly Muslims wanted to be in Pakistan and naturally he, his family and friends decided to migrate there as well. How he reached there is another difficult story since it was the biggest migration of mankind on earth to date, and he was one of the luckiest survivors or the victim of that migration. I am not going to write about that horrific story of the migration as we all know there was a lot of bloodshed and degradation of human lives and no historian can deny these facts.

When he arrived in Pakistan he had to find a place to live as did everyone else. Since it was hard for the authorities to know who was the right candidate and who was forging, they introduced the rule that people coming from the former India had to provide some sort of legal proof. In this way their properties back in India could be evaluated and they could be allotted equivalent places in Pakistan. Actually there was another reason for this control because there were so many people already living in Pakistan who were using their contacts to provide false documents to get as many places as they could. We can see in Pakistan that there are many capitalists and feudalists till today who had obtained many places and now they are one of the richest people in the country. At the same time there are millions who do not even have rooms for shelter. It is a very devastating fact that people are abusing their own people even by knowing that they are in trouble. And this is happening everywhere in the world even today. I have heard this many times and observed it in almost every place where I have lived. Anyway coming back to my point of view, the people therefore had to produce proof of their previous status and properties so they could claim for their places.

He automatically turned to his brother-in-law and asked him about the property which he had bought during his service. He wanted to know whether he had brought the documents with him or had left them behind, since at that time many people were being robbed during the journey. It was hard for everyone to keep their assets as they wanted to secure their lives first and foremost. Of course everyone will do the same thing in such a situation when one has to fight for one's survival. The hardest thing that he came to know, was that his brother-in-law had managed to bring all the legal papers to Pakistan but none of them contained his name. Therefore he had no legal proof of his owning anything over there, whereas his brother-in-law made all the claims and got places for himself and for his other family members. After knowing the facts he was devastated and felt torn and completely shattered. He had nowhere to go and no one to blame but himself as his own family member had cheated and abused his love and trust. Had his brother-in-law forgotten the registration documents in India or they had been stolen, he might have consoled himself in so many other ways. Also there were many other people who were in the same situation and had incurred losses, and most of them did manage to reestablish their lives and go further on. But he did not recover because he was stunned by the fact that the person who was supposed to be his loyal relative, was in fact his enemy and had actually been a snake in the grass.

Now love converted to hate which is quite natural in such cases. His hatred was so deep that it extended even to his race. Whenever he came across any person belonging to his creed he reacted in a very hostile way and he did not explain the reasons. He wanted to cover himself but the wound was so deep that he could not help himself to get over it. He told me himself that even if a beggar, who belonging to the same part of the country as his brother-in-law, ever came up to him he would never ever give him a single penny. After listening to this statement I felt sorry for him but I started thinking that he might have gone a bit too far. But at the same time I could visualize the pain he had being going through in his whole life.

Let us be very honest in judging whether his pain was due to hate, betrayal or discrimination. If anyone who did not know his pain would see him behaving with these people so irrationally, he, I would say, would think that he was discriminating or being a racist and all the other relevant words. But infect it was not discrimination, he was just a victim and was looking for help. But he did not know from whom he might get help. He knew deep inside that he needed help, sometimes he did not even know what he was doing and whether it was just a reflex action. Let us suppose if everyone rebelled against his actions or ideas nobody would find the proper solution. There is no point to hurt those people who have already been hurt enough in all their lives.

People like him need to be loved and someone has to be bold enough to say, yes I am there for you and will mind you, rather than to keep criticizing them. If we keep blaming them then the debate will be almost never ending since both the parties have valid excuses. We sometimes need to reach the bottom of the problem so that the solution can be found. If for a moment we consider this as an example and see what is happening around the world nowadays where everyone is blaming each other for discrimination and classification, and actually no one is takes the time to sit and think rationally about who is wrong and what is the root of the problem. There must be so many children like him in this world who are brought up in some sort of similar situation and are being abused in one way or another. There is no point to keep blaming those who were sufferers and are suffering, it is a time of acceptance and reconciliation rather than neglect. It is very easy to blame people and give them different sorts of titles but it is hard to love people and accept them the way they are. Do we not have to show our good character first rather than to criticize others?

WHAT IS TRUTH

FROM THE LAST FEW DECADES we have been hearing and seeing the social and economic problems of most of the Third world countries. There have been many instances of famines and other disasters which have resulted in the loss of many precious lives. The Western world has watched all these problems and is trying to help those countries as much as possible. During my traveling to a few western countries I discussed this matter with the people to get to know their true thoughts and feelings. I got a very healthy response from most of the people I met. They showed great concern for the situations and the people incurring the disasters, and actively contributed to the funds for the rescue operations. Many organizations are also working to collect funds and send them to the relevant countries where help and food is mostly needed. By seeing only this side of the picture, one would say that Westerners are very loving and understanding and they do feel the pain of the rest of the world. One can also say that they are behaving like a good boss should.

But there is another side to this picture, like in most situations negative and positive go together, such is the case in this particular situation as well. When the same people migrating to the Western world are facing a lot of classification and discrimination, it is hard for them to understand positive aspects which they had heard so much about, for now when they are practically in the situation and interacting with them directly, they are behaving otherwise. Such people then cannot understand the reality, and they are psychologically forced to make many ambiguous statements about the culture which most of the time is based on anger rather than reality. What they cannot figure out is that in their own countries they had heard a lot of positive things about them and the general impression was that the Westerners show utmost concern for the needy people of the needy countries. Also, what they do not understand is that there are many organizations as well who are actively working against them. These organizations do not encourage expatriates, and naturally organizations are run by the people and for the people, that is why there are so many supporters who do not really like foreigners. Though they do not state their views directly or openly since it is not allowed in most of the Western countries especially after the Nazis' behavior in the Second world war, still one can instinctively feel the difference.

Now what is really an amazing fact; the definition of the foreigner is very peculiar in the Western world. Mostly if one is living in a country which is not one's own homeland that will be a foreign land for oneself, and then one is a foreigner in that particular place, but that is not what is meant in the Western world. If an European migrates to another Western country, should that person be called a foreigner in the country where his status is as an immigrant? I would certainly say on paper yes, but otherwise no! In the Western world two terminologies are very commonly heard; foreigners and other countries' people. Foreigner is the title bestowed to those people coming from the Third world, East Europe and South America. The rest of the people belonging to the Western world are treated simply as other country people because they are not alien to each other's culture.

Of course there is no certain way to classify who falls into the category of a foreigner and when to use this term but one can sense very quickly. A Westerner going to another Western country would be treated differently than an Easterner going to that Western country. All Easterners can distinctively smell the difference from the behavior and attitude of the Westerners. An Easterner would be considered a foreigner in the European countries, but not an American, Canadian or even an Australian. Why it is like that I do not know! But what I have observed and seen is that people from the Eastern world enter the Western world with the thought of getting what they can, and they feel no hesitation to cross the prescribed boundaries whereas the fellow Westerner would not think that way in most of the situations. So they are exactly getting what they are sowing. Now do they have a right to blame? Are they speaking the truth?

Of course we know that some people have an attitude towards the people from the troubled countries; but on the other hand, a lot of Western authorities and organizations are working to help the same people in their own countries. Here, a big and very important question arises - What is the truth? Do these people really care for humanity or is this just a whim on the part of the advanced countries to be more popular and control the other part of the world. For normally a rich person, to be more popular and famous, donates huge amounts of money to the welfare organizations. Such people often do it only to be in the news and have their big photographs in the newspapers and on television. Are they using the media for their own purposes? It is certainly a very noticeable point that a certain class of people are helping others just from the marketing point of view. This is their major priority in life, to be more famous and popular. It could be that all the Western countries are trying to outwit each other and show themselves to be more rich and popular, by giving more financial aid in order to have a psychological lead among the other countries. The truth is everybody would love to be superman, but it is nicer when someone is bearing the cost directly or indirectly to genuinely reach out to the people for their welfare and recovery.

NO BLAME GAME

L ATELY WE HAVE SEEN THAT nature was not happy with us and many natural rumps have occurred around the world. It could be an earthquake in Kashmir or hurricane Katrina in America, bushfire in Australia or wind storms here in our beloved land The Netherlands. But one thing is sure that nature is quite unpredicted like our political system and politicians these days. We may call it global warming or it could be alarm signals from God.

Though as humans we presume to know everything and have solutions for all, yet it is beyond to our approach to protect our self from real natural disasters. This has prompted me to think there must be a power above us which keeps examining us from time to time and keep sending indications to us that there is lot more than what a human being can think.

God has made every one of us with a unique identity and qualities and believe me; everyone has his own purpose and mission in this world no matter who; be it Sadam Hussain or Geert Wilders, George Bush or Milosevic. Everyone has their own programme and characteristics and have done their utterly best to let the world be acquainted with their school of thought and as the ultimate resolution for others. But mores the pity that others do not have much to say. In general, innocent people become victims due to such rigid and cruel policies and visions.

My son asked me, *"Papa; why has God created bad people?"*, as I normally advocate on positive attitude and constructive behaviour. He said, "God loves us, then how come bad people?" Understanding his fear and realizing his concern, I have tried to make him apprehend the notion - *"what we think for a while is bad may not be as bad in the long run."* Human perception is restrained, above all there is always a hidden and in some cases open message for others. That is how God communicate with his people. That is his way showing love and kindness toward us.

Believing in religion as I do, at the same time I believe religious cults have somehow gone too far in the race to believe that they are better than others and then they give space to people like Geert Wilders and Robert Mugabe to dig in and misuse the whole system , which is in some way comprehensible as well. The moment one will leave a gap, air will pass through, don't blame air, and fix the opening first.

In a civilised democratic society, everyone has the right to say and communicate his point of view. That's the beauty of such humanity and it is up to others to determine their destiny. However, if the role models themselves are corrupt, after that, one has no option left than just to choose best out of bad bargain.

I would reasonably say to get out of the blame game and find out the solution at grass-root level. Do follow your own religious fundamental norms and ethics rather than to criticise others' values. People who follow their religion truly in fact have very little say to criticise and hate other fellow human being. Given that none of the religions approve violence and killing of innocent human beings.

That is one of our political scenarios nowadays here in Holland and around the world it looks like politicians come and go. I would prefer to bear people like the current Dutch politician Geert Wilders; to let them speak out in order to show the world how they can contribute positively in any society, instead of letting them suppress their ideas and giving them more resistance. Such politicians look like natural disaster; they come and *make the society extinct.*

They say "barking dogs seldom bite": such politicians have a very short term agenda. Therefore the caravan should not worry about their journey and ought to go on. Good work needs to be done, positive minds have to re-gather their point of views and look for productive world for others.

I am strong supporter of high-tech techniques and knowledge. I reckon we have to make every effort to make the world a better place for us. It could be an electronic chip in every human being or any digital device for each of us but we have to make sure that people do not become innocent sufferers and each of us will get equal rights as our beloved religions preach. Love for all and hatred for none, it seems easier said than done.

I hope one day we will establish a system where everyone can live merrily. I have no problem whatsoever if criminals get their own share, nevertheless I do have problem if other sophisticated world has to bother about their deeds. I hope information technology will play a positive role in spreading positive news around the world. We have to know how to distinguish between news and junk and make our boundaries clear on what sort of society do we really want for our forthcoming generation. I thoroughly believe we have to think a little bit broader than just our own house fences. I can reassure you that there are lots and lots of beauty of life yet to explore.

POWER OF LOVE AND CONCORD

W HEN YOU VISIT SOMEONE'S HOUSE you do not have to break the door or enter from the back doors. There are certain codes of conduct and decorum which every society has made and developed for their convenience. Being a civilized human and a good guest, one always has to try to abide to those rules and leave a good impression to the host. As a result they can develop some kind of bond together.

I would say the same rule does apply for those who visit a different country or a different culture. Actually, they are the ambassadors of their countries. Though they might not have the official status but one should always feel like that. That is one of the best opportunities and way to leave an impact on others. It can be positive as well as negative. It is far too difficult when one has inherited a bad name or reputation. What we need to change is the flow of thought. What we need is the young blood to believe in themselves in addition to a positive approach which would lead them somewhere.

Imagine sitting in your living room when someone knocks at your door. Once you open the door you come across someone ill mannered who talks piercingly to you. How long would you bear this sort of behaviour? You had not invited him hence he has no right whatsoever to interact in such an aggressive way. It would not, thus, take you long to shut the door in his face and try to break all sorts of contact with such a person.

This could possibly be the school of thought which different advanced countries are applying nowadays on immigrants. They do not have enough energy or de cliché word "tolerance" left for immigrants. Their 'cup' is full. Since the idea of emigrating is neither providing them peace of mind nor soothing their thoughts. On the contrary, it is causing them headaches and, trust me, no one would like to have headaches. We have to find a correct 'medicine' for their headaches. We have to provide a proper solution for their problem and accordingly we have to correct our approaches as well.

When I mean we have to correct ourselves, the question would then arise; would they accept us? Would there be harmony among us? The answer is **YES**. Have you ever heard of the maxim 'charity begins at home"?. Make sure, if you know better and you behave better as well, in that case, trust me you will find this world full of good people. They will respect you and love you in the same way you behave towards them. By this way actually you are providing them with food for thought which presents to them peace and harmony. Actually you are letting them see the other side of the coin which they have not seen before - the side where respect and love has more value then materialism. Make sure love has more deeper roots than any material thing on this earth. No doubt it has a more positive approach along with consistence required.

Nowadays what an immigrant ought to do is to practically show their behaviour full 360 degrees angle as opposite to the what so-called First world people are thinking about them. The image existing nowadays of the general immigrant has not come from Mars or Venus. It is sad to say it is and was through our own elders. It could be their short sightedness or they might not have seen beyond then their own needs. This is one of the major reason of the traumatic experiences faced by the emigrant today..

Nevertheless, being positive-oriented person, I believe in people power as being great power. Moreover if they want, they can change the directions of the tides the way they want it. But we need to have look for some positive doers who can show the world other side of the coin as well.

How? It is very easy if all of us try to behave and check their own weaknesses and eventually try to rectify them as well. Since that is one of the major characteristics that a successful person needs. I even believe if one us will try to do this, he or she will leave a good impact on others. At that moment people can start developing their own network. A network where respect for others and harmony has ample of space.

I reckon there are certain norms what every immigrant has to try. We have to solve this issue or I may can call it a problem of micro level.. It is not for nothing that this saying exists "penny wise pound foolish". I am a strong believer of the fact that if the basics are healthy and strong then we could build a positive and healthy society as well.

Don't forget once you are in new country behave like as if you are visiting your best friend's house where you always do your best to leave a good name and reputation. If all of us experience immigration this way then I am confident it will not be too far when a migrant would find more friends than enemies. They will receive more love from others then they are used to, especially nowadays!

In a healthy society every positive move and action has an equal and opposite reaction and sometimes more then what one expects. In conclusion I would say, my friends please do good and behave good.

RESPECT FOR ALL

I T IS VERY INTERESTING THAT the people I have met in different parts of the world have asked me in their own way if I am familiar with certain aspects about their culture and country; moreover I have perceived that they felt somehow honoured if I listened to them and do certain stuff the way they have used to. I am, was and will always be a strong believer of the saying "Do in Rome as the Romans do". Therefore I have tried my utter best to adapt what really convinced me and did everything to comfort others and above all, that way I have respected others' norms and values. I must confess that has made my life very easy too.

Currently living here in Holland as I am, I came across people from different ethnic groups and I am forced to write that these people somehow are too proud of their own race or culture with the result they have decided not to bend their routines of life. By doing that they are sending the wrong message to others that they are not accommodating them.

You know! what I have experimented - I have tried to reach people from different cultures; though they came from different parts of the world yet I have noticed certain features which really fascinated me which I would like to share with readers. It was very eminent if I talk their language and try to adapt to their certain lifestyle, they were ready to do and give you everything what one human can possibly expect from a fellow human being. Yet, they were simultaneously not that keen to know more about my background. That behaviour doesn't really bother me. It was at the back of my mind: if you know better then behave better, may be these people might not have sufficient openings or chances in their lives to explore more than what they really know!

I remember I was in Sydney and living in a youth hostel sharing a room with an Irish guy. I had no idea whatsoever about Irish culture except, of course, a certain bookish knowledge about the culture and race. It was very hard to cope with him and share room with him. He did have his own way of living and he grew up in an altogether different world than me. My brought-up in Pakistan was in a very strict and disciplined environment. Consequently it was hard for me to deal with his certain habits, nevertheless at the same time, I did not have any other option; not having enough money to live on my own made me to go for the challenge. I eventually started understanding his state of affairs and learned more about his norms and values.

The hostel where we were staying was not just Irish; it was full of a mixed creed of people. Hence, if I managed to adjust with my room mate, I would still come across others in the laundry room or washroom which I was not accustomed to. To make a long story short it took me about six months to settle myself and I worked everyday and night to make it happen. Personally I am goal-oriented: I gave myself a challenge and then made every effort to let it happen.

I had started leaning Irish dialect and had managed to touch the heart of the people. Believe it or not, after learning just one sentence of their language I was nicely welcomed in the group that is my manner of digging in and to manage to develop a very strong acquaintance with the people for which I am till today proud of. That was my start at living on my own and that was the response of my initiative and that has motivated me throughout my career. I must say it was really worth it. I have learned many positive aspects of life and my behaviour towards foreigners became more friendly.

Now after fifteen years and having seen, in the meantime, many more countries and making friends from diverse cultures and backgrounds, I feel very proud, somehow, blessed that I have received a lot of respect and love from people. It has helped me, on a daily basis, to make my belief stronger and stronger.

As we know from the last five years or so the world has changed. It is not only here in Holland, it is everywhere and there is no one to blame but ourselves. We are all contributors whether it be actively or passively. Sometimes passive behaviour can be more dangerous - by keeping eyes shut and expecting that everything will be all right and 'will never happen to me' is not a good approach either. This kind of behaviour helps the evil effectively, that is what they wanted; to create hate and fear among human beings and cultures. I would be the last person to give up. I reckon it is in fact time to show behaviour than to keep pointing out others' faults.

It is a time for people to show their deeds and positive behaviour and of course "it take two to quarrel", therefore we need to support people who are really making an effort and spending their time for good conduct. Of course you can change direction of the trends if you really desire to, in addition to contributing actively and positively. The moment you begin to defend and go for shielding arguments then mostly somehow somewhere things do not flow smoothly.

As we know, birds of a feather flock together, however, that does not mean that they should be having the same colour as well. It can be more versatile, plus it would be nicer if they are from everywhere and anybody can join them as long as they share the same school of thoughts. Believe it or not, that will stimulate more love and respect in the air for each other.

I am not expecting from people to transform their identities and forget about their own upbringing and roots, no, on the contrary, what I am suggesting is to expand your horizon and give and take more space for yourself -that can be very constructive, make no mistake. If u are ready to respect others' feelings and traditions, it is then that you will actually be able to communicate and acknowledge your point of view as well. Predominantly, I have observed there are much more confusions than the real specifics.

In the history of time, people have been migrating from one place to another and have later on decided to settle down in their chosen land for good. Being at first, settlers or migrants, they go on to achieve the status of owners or natives of the country. It happened in the past and it can happen in the future as well. Everywhere, the only approach that actually works is a positive attitude and respect for your fellow human being. I would say please care for each other and live for each other.

I am not expecting people to leave their communities and start integrating for others, what I am signifying that could be the way they might feel more comfortable too. Sometime while comforting others you can find more peace and prosperity. By doing that you pass positive vibrations to others and that can be and is a good contribution for creating a healthy society.

I am a strong believer in the fact that if everyone starts behaving good towards each other; the way he or she wants to be treated. It will not be too long that we will be enjoying a good atmosphere around us and that way we can protect our human values which are in fact more stronger than cultural values.

UNITED WE STAND

I T IS THE BEGINNING OF a new year and I am taking the privilege to wish you all a very happy, healthy and united 2008. In everyone's life many things happened in 2007; try to be honest with yourself and learn from your mistakes in order to attain a prosperous start.

The idea is not to discuss the facts and figures of the previous year - that can be attained from Google or some other source. What inspires me is "life" itself and I believe it to be the greatest gift bestowed on us by God. Every possible thing associated with human beings inspires me, be it religion, culture or customs.

We have to learn how to celebrate unity – the concept and spirit of togetherness. As we know celebration is the finest way to express joy and happiness as well as on the other hand to be thankful of what we have. We must consider the limitations as it should not be by any means at the cost of others. It may be the achievements of your kids, a festival day or fireworks at New Year's Eve.

Talking about fireworks, I was really astonished at the mega total of losses incurred this year. The approximate estimation is about 120 millions; only 16 million people have burned 120 for just a few hours' lust. I am still struggling at this perception of real celebration. Is this the real notion of festivity and enjoyment; to burn children's schools and cars of fellow humans? If this is that we define as celebration then with all honesty it doesn't make any sense to me.

For people to get together at one place and enjoy firework with reasonable quantity is logical, however I don't understand when it becomes a hype or the fact that everyone has to buy as much as they want for the purpose of creating noises harder and louder just to impress their mates or neighbors as well as to prove that they are the best along with having unsurpassed firework. I would rather choose to be the best through another manner and style than through all my money being spent on firework.

When I heard about the cancellation of New Year's Eve celebration this year in Brussels I was very happy for a while. At least one nation had chosen not to waste money - or so I thought optimistically. Once I came to know the reason I felt regret. That it is not the way to live in a healthy society either. Where a certain thick headed and negative-minded group is dreaming to threaten the fate of civilized people and decided to change the world through harassment. That is not a healthy and adequate way either to function in the healthy society.

We have to negate them as much as we can with our positive actions. I strongly believe if someone abuses you and you abuse them back then there will be no difference among them and they may not be able to solve anything. On the other hand that might create another chaos. It seems wiser to me if one party behaves better and avoids conflicts. It becomes easier for others to judge and choose for the peace.

Whilst discussing this issue in my surrounding, I noted an interesting fact - I somehow didn't come across many who were against the idea of buying fireworks. Mostly people had spent a few Euros on these low explosive pyrotechnic devices and that should not have any consequences. Which I thoroughly understand and it defiantly seems good sense to me as well. In reality, though, these few euros are a little bit too much and at the end of the day the sad conclusion is: a country of 16 million people has deficit of around 120 million. And surely, that is for me an alarming issue.

In the aftermath of natural disastrous situations occurring globally, the western countries send their aids to the developing world which amount to 5 millions or 10 millions. Imagine if we could just contain our joy and festivity for a while, how much productive we could be for the billions of kids lacking proper nutrition, an adequate place to live and the other basic necessities of life which is their due human right. We might be able to help change their fate and make the world better place to live for every person.

We have to feel blessed that we have the facilities to live a better life and enjoy our lives the way we want it. There is no harm to spend just a few amount for others' welfare as well. Every one of us living in Holland is Dutch and each one of us is equally responsible for our own deeds. We have to learn how to think collectively and for that we have to act collectively.

Make sure every deed has its own repercussions and definitely helping each other will help us to make the world better place. Like John F. Kennedy said "Ask not what your country can do for you - ask what you can do for your country." We have to learn to contribute rather than to pin point others. I am sure we all can do something to make a difference. As a matter of fact at the end of the day obviously it would be good for the country, good for the respective economy and above all good for mankind. Think about it!

www.ingramcontent.com/pod-product-compliance
Lightning Source LLC
Chambersburg PA
CBHW020441290526
45785CB00002B/962